Threads

A journey into the picture of the soul

Judith Cosby
8/17/19

JUDITH COSBY

Cover Design by Ana Grigoriu–Voicu, Books Design.

Editing by Veronica Jordan, Storyteller Alley

Author Photo by Scott Peloquin, The 413 Photography.

Proofreading by Vickie Wiechec, Vickie Wiechec @Associates

ISBN-13: 978-0-692-04207-6 (print book)

ISBN-10: 0-692-04207-5 (print book)

ASIN: B07JQNZX8Z (KDP e-book)

10 9 8 7 6 5 4 3 2 1

1. Spirituality 2. Self Help 3. New Age 4. Memoir 5. Inspiration 6. Supernatural 7. Empowerment

First Edition

Visit my website at www.judithcosby.com

"Paradise has never been about places. It exists in moments. In connection. In flashes across time."

~ Victoria Erickson

Table of Contents

DEDICATION/ACKNOWLEDGEMENTS

I dedicate this book to those who championed and inspired me to follow my heart and write THREADS. I thank you for the blessing of being a part of my journey.

To the friends in my life who never ceased to share their encouragement and support: Vickie, Lisa, Brenda, and Julie, you were my cheerleaders.

To my fellow authors who shared their knowledge and wisdom of the literary world: Suzanne McKenna Link and Kevin Bezner, my respect and appreciation are boundless.

To my editor Veronica Jordan of Storybook Alley, who encouraged me to push through many of my stories with richer meaning. I appreciate your professionalism and your kindness.

A very special thank you to my husband, Craig Cosby, and my mother, Shirley Ribeiro, for your constant love, direction, and belief in my dream.

To my daughters, Sarah and Catherine, for your endless inspiration. You both are my world.

To my father, Joaquim Ribeiro, who never had the opportunity to know I accomplished this endeavor, but who nurtured me in my early years and never stopped believing in me. His tether remains even from beyond this world to allow me to see that our picture never really ends, just weaves into a different form.

And I thank God, for bestowing upon me the gift of writing, the courage to follow my dream, and the wisdom to believe that all things are possible in His name.

THE BEGINNING

"I know that every single encounter, every challenge, and every situation are all spectacular threads in the tapestry that represents and defines my life, and I am deeply grateful for all of it."

~ *Dr. Wayne Dyer*

Too often we only examine our life in retrospect. We use the benefit of hindsight to contemplate our past motivations and glean meaning from our previous struggles. For many, the patterns of our lives appear as only random zigzags of emotion and knowledge. But what if, armed with the simple understanding that our lives are a complex and beautiful tapestry of experiences and connections, we could learn how to alter our paths and better understand our own unique purpose?

The idea of *Threads* came to me one day while I was attending Sunday mass. I was a young woman, fresh out of high school, and pursuing my own personal religious journey at that time. I made a habit of attending Sunday sermons in my small hometown church of Feeding Hills, Massachusetts. My freshman year of college was on the horizon and I found that our priest's sermons were comforting and inspirational as I began my passage into adulthood.

As I waited for the sermon to begin, sunlight streamed through the arc of stained glass windows that spanned the front wall of the church. Sitting alone in the light oak pew I was captivated by the brilliance of light and splash of color that fell upon the altar. A rainbow of refracted hues dotted the group of communicants. It wasn't the first time this phenomenon had caught my attention. Almost every sunny Sunday morning bore witness to this same miracle of color and light within the sanctuary. In the summer, the effect was almost magical. The colors would fall on various members as they sat in the pews and I would sit in awe of its beauty. In my mind, the individuals that the colors landed on were special somehow, maybe even touched by God. I found the purple to be the most beautiful, and at times, the most spiritual. I hoped it would someday land on me.

My senses fully engaged, and my heart open to the guidance his sermon promised, I listened intently to the words of Father Joyce. As he stood at the pulpit, his tall, thin stature and kindly face were bathed in purple light. His gentle voice began to speak of scripture and of the ethereal world. He spoke about a grand scale tapestry that was constantly being created and how our lives intermingled with others to form one great masterpiece. He spoke specifically about our own tapestries, and how, at the end of our lives, long or short, it would be a beautiful piece of work to behold.

As he continued, I watched the light and colors dance and sway across the congregation with warmth and vibrancy. The scattering of color blanketed various members with light, occasionally shifting to include the person at their side or the ones in front or behind them. I was intrigued by the concept that just the shift of the sun or the movement of clouds could change how many individuals were touched at the same moment. It was then that I began to understand that at any given time, and in any venue or situation, we all possess the opportunity to connect with others in a positive or negative fashion.

This discovery became the inspiration of my life. I knew that by imagining the colors, textures, and patterns of my threads, the threads that were woven into the tapestry Father Joyce had spoken about, and by understanding the lessons and emotions associated with each strand, I could improve my life. In time, I became inspired to share this idea with others in hopes that it could be a beneficial tool and one that many could relate to.

"Threads" is a concept that does not require deep introspective thought, but it does offer a uniquely powerful way to create the life we envision for ourselves. Visualizing the colors and textures of our actions and viewing them in a positive way enables us to mold our lives into a grand scale tapestry that reflects, not only those moments of our past, but also the brilliant existence that is our present. It is an idea, however, that requires an openness of thought and an acceptance that our actions and reactions have an impact on the lives we touch and the paths we take. It enables us to contemplate how our interactions, emotions, and relationships are depicted in one grand picture instead of a series of random events connected only by the progression of time.

When identifying with the threads concept, we begin to realize how important it is to not only fashion a life that makes us feel good about ourselves but also reflects positively upon our fellow man. It demonstrates how the use of positive words and kind actions, not only enhances the lives around us, but also makes our own lives positively fulfilled.

Life can be a beautiful portrait. It is an intricately woven, spectacular tapestry that can reflect the simplest or deepest of moments and spans into the infinite vastness of the universe. It not only tells our own individual stories, but also connects and interweaves with those of others. It is composed of the most beautiful colors and designs. It is the creation of the most exquisite threads and uniquely personal workmanship. Even the threads composed of the darkest colors emit a light. This radiant light represents the eternal light of our soul.

The threads that form our creations all have their own gifts. For within each thread, in each weave, there is a texture, a color, a feeling, and a meaning. The feelings are for various reasons and represent moments of joy, love, loss, and so on.

As we age, and our lives become more fragile, the tapestry threads may become coarser and weathered with the passage of time, but the strength and the color never wane or lose their luster.

Some tapestries are not as elaborate, and some are hardly made. Those are the lives that may not have finished their work or were cut off too early, but their own personal light added a texture, a color, and a feeling to those it touched. There are other tapestries that have been given the benefit of a long and profound life. They are almost masterpieces of their own making. Whether long or short, each strand of every tapestry elicits the chance for life to grow and become part of the grand, cosmic picture.

This book seeks to share my understanding of the threads and how they have and are creating my life. As you read, I invite you to embrace the idea that you possess a beacon that is uniquely your own. And though that light may burn brilliantly at times, or glow softly at others, it always illuminates an incredible picture of your life force and all those you touch with it.

VISUALIZING YOUR TAPESTRY

"Life is a blank canvas, and you need to throw all the paint on it you can"

~ *Danny Kaye*

We are all composed of the same threads, regardless of the color of our skin, our faith, or our gender. It is what we do with our weaves and our tapestries that help create the uniqueness of our lives. Once you begin to acknowledge and utilize the colors and threads of your tapestry, you can then begin to apply that understanding to your everyday life. It is not difficult. It simply requires conscious intent. When you awake to embrace your day, visualize how you would like it to appear. Imagine the colors, the threads and the components that you will use to transform the blank canvas of the next twenty-four hours.

To begin, it is important to consider your composite thread. It is the thread that we are innately made from: the first thread, the strand that was developed right from birth. It is pure and untouched. It is you before all of the other threads began to bind. This composite thread was so pure that it was a flicker of light in the darkness. It never felt happiness, sadness, acceptance, rejection, glory, or pain. It was just a pure light before the world surrounded it to begin your tapestry. Its initial weave is driven by your DNA combined with all of the love and guidance from those in your life.

To conceptualize it we must really delve into who we are. What we must ask ourselves is what really lies within our body and soul makeup? We all have interests and dislikes and paths taken and avoided, but that is not all of who we are. Compassion, empathy, drive, and love have an influence. When going inside our self and picturing those fundamentals of who we are, a glimpse of the composite thread is captured.

If you are reading this book, there is a spiritual nature about you that allows you to be open to the thought process of this concept. That may be a portion of your composite thread, the spiritual drive inside of you.

No matter what your first thread is composed of, close your eyes and imagine how you have developed that essence of you to this day. Your vision of your tapestry can grow from there, and can be incorporated into your daily routine.

As you begin to visualize your day, be conscious of your words, actions, and deeds. Every one of these has an outcome and an influence on not only our day, but in the collective journey of others. Although humans are never perfect, the idea of weaving your threads and allowing them to touch and be a part of other tapestries in the kindest of fashions is the goal of the masterpiece.

Create your beautiful masterpiece by choosing the color and threads of your day, and in the process, your life. Every path, decision, and act produces a thread. The tapestry is ever growing. The colors, the uniqueness of the threads in their heft and weight, and the simplicity or complexity of the design are the unifying force. Emotions provide a richness of colors.

It is important to remember that in everyday life, while there is the mundane and the routine, there is also always a gift. Small and large miracles are available to all. Focus on creating your day with a calm and kind demeanor, even through the most difficult of moments. When the challenging times come, and the very concept of calm seems unattainable, take a deep breath and trust that there is a thread of a blessing in every single day. Even in the darkest of times, gifts emerge to ease or lighten our hearts. Be diligent in your search and recognition of these miracles. Do not get lost in the darkness, but allow the light and hope to enter into your world. Walk a path that is cognizant of these gifts and you will rarely miss the wonderful things around you.

The beauty of this concept has allowed me to envision exactly how my own tapestry is designed and seems to flow. Ever since I began to imagine my life in the form of threads, colors, and weaves, it has added another dimension to how I see things and handle all kinds of situations. It has made my heart kinder and my expressions softer. Viewing life and death has become a different picture for me. This concept is not a perfect ideal that explains all facets of our vitality, but it does allow us to rationalize the concept of how we would like the design to be sewn into our fabric of life.

I prefer to keep the vision of my tapestry more traditional and colorful, almost like a scrapbook. It brings forth an image of so many wonderful moments and experiences. The magical thing about being able to visualize your tapestry is that it is completely yours and therefore has a uniqueness about it that is as singular and rare as you are. We are creative and accepting of what life has given us. From those threads, we then create images and moments that become the memories we will recall as we move forward in our lives.

Every masterpiece is like a fingerprint, each is one-of-a-kind. The size of the tapestry is not just measured by the length of life, but also by the vitality of the soul. Personal and spiritual growth and acts of kindness all influence the depth and width of the masterpiece.

The tapestry itself is a spiritual vision and can take many forms. It is the perception of the soul that creates the masterpiece and allows the colors and shapes to emerge. The colors are unique to each tapestry and are created daily as are the threads that weave it. Some tapestries will emerge with a mosaic pattern, with bold lines and geometric shapes, all created by the paths that one takes. Other tapestries may be created in quilt form, woven in squared sections that reflect one period at a time, and then are merged together. Another form could look more like a work of art or painting. It could be a grand picture of the person, the details fashioned by all of the journeys he or she experienced in life. There is no right or wrong in how our tapestries appear. The idea is to see in our mind what we would like our picture to be and then begin to weave.

THE THREADS OF POWER

"In the midst of winter, I found there was, within me, an invincible summer."

~ *Albert Camus*

The summer after I turned twelve should have been filled with all of the things summers promise like ice cream cones, hanging with your friends, and swimming in the neighborhood pool. But instead, I spent the summer afraid of a bully, choosing to sequester myself inside my house rather than risk running into her.

Dana was three times my size and three years older than me. She lived in another neighborhood and would ride her ten-speed bike up and down my street at various times of the day spouting off threats of beatings. There were times, while my parents were at work and I was home alone, that she and her friends would come to my house and bang on the windows and doors and yell threats at me. I sat in my house terrified.

I really did not know my bully and was, through no fault of my own, the victim of guilty-by-association. For a few weeks at the beginning of the summer, a cousin from the eastern part of Massachusetts had come to visit with my family. She was a very mature and worldly 15-year-old girl, who wore very stylish clothes and spoke with a Boston accent. She had a beautiful figure, olive colored skin that tanned to perfection and long, curly brown hair. Her eyes were gorgeous — deep brown and surrounded by lush dark lashes. I was in complete adoration of her and all of the neighborhood boys were intrigued by her. One boy, in particular, paid more than normal attention to her and she liked it. Unfortunately, this boy happened to have dated Dana's best friend. It would seem that my bully took great offense to this behavior and when my cousin left to return home, Dana decided I would have to pay.

I kept this horrible secret to myself for as long as I could. No one in my family and none of my friends knew of the torment I was enduring. One afternoon, my two best friends, Christine and Pauline, who lived a mile from my house, asked me to meet them in the center of town for snacks and soda. They pleaded with me over the phone to come and hang out. I had put them off so many times that I had run out of excuses and finally disclosed my dirty little secret.

I told them I was petrified to leave my house and walk alone down the main road to the center of town for fear I would run into Dana and her friends. My two friends both promised to meet me halfway and assured me that there was nothing to fear for they would be on either side of me. The thought of spending the day with them was enticing and at that moment, I trusted that they would keep me from harm.

Anxious to meet my friends, I quickly dressed and got myself ready to go. I grabbed my chore money and hurried out the front door. I phoned both of my friends to tell them I was leaving my house and they agreed to meet me halfway as promised. In my mind, our plan was brilliant and very well thought.

I hurried out my front door, stepped out into the street, and scanned the cul-de-sac and its only exit for the fated ten-speed bike. I had already created numerous scenarios in my mind of what I would do to protect myself, where I would go and hide, and speculated how fast I really could run should the need arise.

I hooked a right off my street onto the moderately busy thoroughfare that led to the main road. I would have to pass three houses and a Dairy Mart to get to the corner. I was convinced that if I could just get through this stretch I was almost guaranteed safety until I met up with my friends on the main road.

As I turned left onto the main road, it occurred to me that there was, however, a tiny snafu in my safety plan. I had not considered how I was going to get home. Cell phones and all the technology that we often take for granted now were non-existent back then. I would have to ask my friends to see me a bit of the way back home to keep me safe.

And then I spied them, two figures on bikes coming up the main road. It was in that moment that I recognized my plight. The evil ten-speed bike was hurdling up onto the sidewalk with my cruel tormentor hunched over its handlebars like the Wicked Witch of the West, along with her meaner flying monkey sidekick. How could this be? I had made it this far, surely my friends must be right behind them. But it was too late. There she was, larger than life. I had nowhere to go. My fear was right in front of me and I was alone, with nowhere to hide. It was then I knew there was nothing else I could do but face her and confront my situation without fear.

They pulled up in front of me, blocking my path before climbing off of their bicycles and setting their kickstands. Their impromptu blockade ensured I could not run any further up the road and they stood before me like two Goliaths before a singular David. Dana was tall for her age and had a large upper body. Her hair was long and thick giving the impression that she was even taller. I was tiny in comparison.

"I thought I warned you I better not ever find you alone," she yelled. "That you shouldn't even be in my sight, or else."

I stood there and just stared at them, not saying a word.

That's when I noticed a nervous glint in her eye.

The two girls shifted a bit and as I stared at her, I watched her expression on her face become anxious, almost pained.

"Do it! Hit her!" screamed Shellie, her sidekick, a very mature-figured 15-year-old with a plain face.

I didn't move, nor did I beg or make a sound.

"It's too... it's too public. I can't do it here," Dana stammered.

But Shellie egged her on repeating the same chant. "Go on, hit her! Do it!"

Over the handlebars of the bicycle blockade, I could see my friends in the far distance. They were walking, but with no sense of urgency. They did not see me amongst the bikes and two larger girls.

The bully approached, and I braced myself and sneered. I held my body rigid for the impact and was ready to take it. I needed to end this. I could tell that she did not want to do it. She was saving face in front of her mean friend.

The massive blow to the side of my face hit me like a ton of bricks. I kept my feet, never saying a word. Never uttering a word of pain or crying out. I stood there, angry but triumphant. I had faced my fear.

Shellie got on her bike and as she began to peddle she slapped my head on the ride by. Dana hefted her overweight body onto her bike and peeled out into the street, the sand under her tires made a grinding sound as she peddled away.

"Watch out," she called over her shoulder as she rode to catch up with her sidekick.

I waited for a moment and then turned to see their Laurel and Hardy frames ride off into the distance. I spun back to see the concerned look on my approaching friends' faces and the tears rolled down my cheeks. My lips quivered and I managed, "it's finally over."

Christine, Pauline, and I had chips, drank sodas, laughed, and talked. When our time was finished, I left them at the center of town and told them I was fine to walk back home by myself. As I retraced my steps back to my house, I was invincible. I had faced my fears and used my power thread to my advantage.

Ironically, years later I injured my arm falling off the steps of our deck and found myself in our local ER. The triage nurse came over to take my vitals and check my hand. The nurse, a large hard-looking woman, started to check my pulse and I then noticed her name badge – Dana.

She looked at me and smiled. "You look familiar, do I know you?"

At the time, I was a 33-year-old mother of two, but for only a split second, I was that 12-year-old girl with a fear of torment in her heart. Then my power thread came back to bolster me. I imagined saying to her, "why yes, you were the 15-year-old bully that ruined a child's summer so long ago." But instead I looked at her and said firmly, "No, I don't think so."

The power thread is a very individual thread and varies from person to person. There are people who become empowered by a cause or crusade and fight for their belief with rigor and determination. The purpose is so great that it emerges into the weave with a glittering fierceness and they do battle with a fortitude they did not believe they were capable of.

Threads

Threads of power add a unique texture to the weave. Every tapestry has its own original blend of colors and textures, but a power thread is defined by its strength and thickness. It is resilient in its makeup. It is the thread that emerges when we need to bolster our picture and find our strength and courage. Understanding this thread and using it at the proper times is exceptionally important. Its most gifted aspect is to grow and strengthen us at times when we are most weak or vulnerable. It is meant to give us the power to conquer our fears, support and protect those things we truly care about, and face the impossible at times when all hope seems lost. To know that we possess such a thread is a blessing and one that will add texture to our final picture.

THE THREADS OF SELF WORTH AND DOUBT

"The heart of man is very much like the sea, it has its storms, it has its tides and in its depths it has its pearls too."

~ *Vincent van Gogh*

At thirteen years of age, I received a diary as a Christmas present from my parents. During that time of my life, I had no interest in writing in a journal about myself. Those early teen years are awkward times with body changes and emotional upheavals. I was a walking, raging hormone, happy one minute, distant and cranky the next. The diary was a bright red leather-bound book with the word *Journal* etched in black on the cover. I was intrigued, but at the time, there were more exciting gifts under the tree such as pieces of jewelry, record albums, and clothes. As the days went on and I had enjoyed those expected gifts, the red journal sat prominently on my yellow antiqued-glazed desk like a beacon waiting for me to come to it.

Several weeks later, I finally gave in to its call and decided to sit down and write something inside. I pulled out my wooden pine chair and sat at my desk. I named my journal and wrote a dedication to her on the first, pristine page. I introduced myself and what I was feeling at that moment, telling my paper confidant what my hopes were for my life. I took the time to write down some of the everyday details of my life, including the number of animals we had and their names. I promised that I would write every day and tell my journal whatever I was thinking.

On the next line I wrote what I hoped for in my future and what I wanted to be... an author.

For almost three years, I wrote in my journal. I recorded special celebrations, daily experiences, and wonderful tidbits that reflected events in my childhood that would have long been forgotten if not recorded. But life twisted and turned and I grew older. Things like friends, Drivers Ed, and boys took over my life. My very last entry was rushed and unthoughtful. I closed my journal and shoved it in the bottom drawer of my desk and never looked back.

For almost thirty-five years the diary lay hidden in a box of personal belongings that was packed away when I redid my room as I entered my college years. The box, emblazoned with the words "Judy's Papers," was then stored in the garage of my new home as I began my life as a married woman and then it took up residence in the basement of my permanent home. As my own children grew and went to college, I began cleaning out the basement and came across my box.

I opened it to find that the inside was musty and covered in dust, like a time capsule of someone I hardly knew anymore. As I unpacked these strange childhood treasures, there lay the beautiful red book. I lifted it out of the box and read through the initial, short passages of what my thirteen-year-old self had felt, dreamed, and hoped for. I sat on the carpeted floor of my finished basement and began to read, laughing and crying over the wonderful surge of memories. I laughed out loud at the innocence and drama of the day. But then I re-read the dedication page of this handwritten treasure and there were those words: "I will write in you every day and share my life with you and follow my dream to someday write a book." I read the words and a spark of desire to reach that goal ignited in my heart.

Unfortunately, I allowed my inner voice to whisper into my mind, "You are not capable of that." Later, I shared my thoughts about writing a book with a few other people. One said, "But you don't have any creative writing schooling." Those feelings and words echoed in my mind and I put down the idea. That little thread of self-doubt tried to sew a permanent stitch into my fabric. But then I began to feel a calling deep within—a feeling of a bigger and greater purpose, of sharing this idea of the connections we make. Regardless of its popularity or its success, I would write a book and become an author. It was as if finding the journal was life's reminder to finish what I had set out to accomplish so long ago.

Funny how what I thought I wanted that Christmas many years before were all material things. But those things usually give a level of joy that is fleeting. My beloved journal had transcended all these years to relay the message. Life had pushed forward, and the dream and the confidence had waned, but the self-worth thread emerged and gave a charge to the present tapestry with a light. The thread was rewoven and gave value to this hopeful author in a segment of her tapestry. I am grateful for that gentle reminder and whether I write one book or ten, the initial drive to create something for others to read is a path I intend to follow, regardless of the doubt I previously placed upon myself.

The threads of self-worth and doubt do link from time to time, but let your self-worth shine and glow and weave the dreams you have envisioned.

In our day-to-day lives, and especially as we age, we incorporate too many threads of doubt into our fabric. They can touch our tapestries and damage them through outside influences or from our own dark places. These threads will, at times, affect how we proceed in our given paths and can even alter what we are capable of weaving in the future.

It is so important to know that we all possess qualities and talents that can lead us to wonderful places if we only have faith in ourselves. Believing in yourself and creating a picture that is everything we have imagined in the future is a gift.

Imagine that inside of all of us is an untapped potential of light. Whether it is as simple as a white light or as broad as a rainbow, it is yours to imagine. The idea is to shine that beacon out to the world so that you can draw the positive threads from it. There will be people who are intimidated by the light you innately shine. They may try to extinguish or dull its brightness, but never let them stop your light from shimmering radiantly.

THE THREADS OF LIFE STAGES

"There is nothing like returning to a place that remains unchanged to find the ways in which you yourself have altered."

~ Nelson Mandela

One unusually cold March day, my mother and I sat chatting about life in the warmth of my kitchen. I put out a plate of Irish cheddar cheese and crackers and poured two hot cups of Red Rose tea.

My mother began to stir the sugar in her tea in a familiar fashion, scraping the bottom of the cup until all of the sugar granules dissolved. It was a familiar and strangely comforting sound. How many times over the course of my life had I heard that same sound as my mom stirred her tea, clinking and scaping her spoon against her Pfaltzgraff tea cup? I looked across my kitchen table and watched the steam rise from our cups, the wispy water vapor mingling together.

As she sipped her tea, my mother shared revelations about the phases of her life. She and I would often discuss our views on many subjects such as politics, relationships, a new TV series, a good book, or just life in general. Lately she had become more introspective about her own life and how the concept of threads had touched her.

"As we age," she said, "we morph into a different version of ourselves. We may experience a similar situation, but we see the value in it differently."

Intrigued with her comment I asked, "Why do you feel that way?"

Her thoughtful gaze focused on me, but I could tell her mind was clearly somewhere in the past.

"As a child I saw things differently," she said. "I often think about my early life back on Tecumseh Street. I wish many times I could go back and appreciate all that I had at the time."

"Were you not happy while you were there?" I questioned.

"My family was poor and my mother very ill for a major portion of my life." She hesitated for a minute as she played with the handle of her tea cup. "My mother died young and my family was never the same," she said sadly.

I could see that these memories were hard for her to recall. I asked, "How did you value things differently than you do now?"

She began to share two examples of how she acknowledged the threads of life stages within her own life. A child of the Great Depression, my mother was the fourth child in an Irish family of seven, born in the mill town of Fall River, Massachusetts.

"When we lived in the tenement, in an apartment on the third floor, my mother kept a fancy living room. Growing up, we were never allowed to sit in that room except for very special occasions. My mother had damask lined drapes and a fancy parlor table in the center of the room. On top of this table she kept a set of six ruby-red sherry glasses with gold stems. In the late afternoon, the sun would stream in through the window and through those glasses."

I could imagine how it must have looked with the splashes of the sunlit red reflections dancing across the cream-colored walls of the room.

My mother smiled as she recalled the sight. "It was breathtaking."

"It's a little funny how precious those sherry glasses were. No one in our family drank, so the glasses were never used."

She went on to tell me how much she had always admired the room but wished they could have celebrated more family moments there.

"I remember the day my brothers and sister and I found fifteen cents on a sidewalk outside our home," she continued, recalling even more about her childhood.

"That money would hardly buy anything today, but back then, it was like finding a fortune. Two of my brothers picked up the change and we ran up the steep stairs to our third-floor apartment. We carefully placed the dime and nickel on the worn oak table and presented it to our mother."

She told me how they had all stared at the two coins as if they had uncovered a buried treasure. As she spoke, I could feel the deep emotions that sprang forth when she thought about that moment from so long ago.

We nibbled on the crackers and cheese, the mist of the tea dissipating between us, and discussed how life had transcended from those years. It was then that she realized the thread of life stages existed for both of us, yet it was differently placed, a different heft, and she had emerged into a level of life I had not reached.

My mother explained that the things she valued and how she valued them had changed.

"I still marvel at the beauty of my mother's living room, but the greatest value is found in the memories of that room, rather than the items within its four walls. Fifteen cents is as important to me now as it was then, but it's not the money itself, or the things I could spend it on, but the idea of sharing the treasure with family that is valuable."

I listened to her explain how she grew and changed with each level of her life and about the thoughts and ideas of the little girl and young teenager she had once been. She described her reflections as the mother and provider I had grown up with, and then as the older woman she was now. Her memories and experiences had not changed, but her understanding of their importance and their role in her life had evolved.

As I listened, I realized I had morphed into another level myself. I was her daughter, but I was also her contemporary, listening to the pearls of wisdom from my sage friend, and engaging in a moment with a woman I was just getting to know, outside of her role as my mother. Our relationship was becoming another phase in our life thread—twisting, knotting, unraveling, and smoothing out as our life threads interlaced for that moment.

The thread of life stages is ever-present. It is there as we begin to learn and understand the world around us and our part in it. In its initial weave, it is the string of newness and innocence, the beginning of our journey on earth. As children, our needs and pleasures are simple. Our tapestries are filled with the weaves and ties from those around us. As our life thread continues, we enter our teenage years and our life thread begins to change. We are carefree and daring. Our creation reflects the energy of youth and endless possibilities. Our thread expands as we are reformed again as young adults, starting out on our own. Our lives are full of new responsibilities and directions. Careers, families, and homes become our new level of life. We are all of those things and more.

Then the weave takes on another direction. We become something older and wiser. We develop a distinct perspective on life and what is important to us. No longer are our careers the priority. Our direction may ebb and flow, but we are silently preparing for the next phase. Our life thread becomes frailer, wider, yet more valuable. We are rich in color, yet less vibrant.

Then we enter the final stage of our life thread. These are the years when we return to our basic self. The weaves are not as widespread. They tend to be more stationary. This is the phase of our long weave where we understand who we are and what we have finally become. By now, our life thread is more of a ribbon than a string and we can see how intricate it has become over the years. We spend more time looking back and less time looking forward. We see that our journey has taken us to so many levels of life. Some brief, some long, some joyous, and some sad.

It is a gift to be able to single out the thread of life stages from the greater picture and really take in its journey and to visualize and acknowledge the many levels of what we were and what we have finally become.

THE THREADS OF INTERTWINING FATES

"Accept the things to which fate binds you, and love the people with whom fate brings you together, but do so with all your heart."

~ *Marcus Aurelius*

Born on a chilly November 5, 1962, I was the first grandchild to my nana, Evangelina. Her husband, my grandfather, Joaquim, had died the previous year and missed meeting his first grandchild, but my nana would often tell me how much my grandfather would have loved me had he had the chance to know me.

Evangelina, my father's mother, was born in Lisbon, Portugal on November 10, 1911, and was the oldest of 8 siblings. She moved to America from Portugal when she was in the third grade. A very beautiful girl with olive skin, thick ebony hair and large brown eyes, she grew up on a small farm in East Providence and lived a very simplistic life. When I knew her as my nana her form was matronly, but in her youth, she had a very voluptuous figure.

Nana was an incredible cook. She was famous in our family and in her community for her Portuguese kale soup with both linguica and chourico, country-style chicken, and her delectable Malassadas dripping with molasses. It was her love of food that makes me love to cook today. I remember sitting on a stool in her tiny kitchen watching her create her culinary masterpieces. That kitchen, so simplistic compared to today's standards, is still, to this day, the one kitchen I would love to be able to cook in again. There were no measuring cups or cookbooks, just an old, white gas stove with a heavy door that groaned every time she opened it and the cast-iron pots that she cooked in. She would add a pinch of this and a pinch of that. Her hands were mesmerizing, working hands that created dishes as if there was magic within those bent fingers.

Although my nana lived in another state and we had to travel for two hours to see her, we were able to visit often and I loved those times with her. Through my adult years, I did not see her as much. My aunt, Nana's only daughter, suffered from mental illness and it affected many family outings and slowly isolated my nana from the world. We spoke often, but we did not physically see each other towards the end of her life.

I was fortunate enough to have my nana until I was 35. On Halloween night in 1999, I had a dream of her. She stood in the doorway of my bedroom, glowing in a shower of white light. She smiled at me and waved her left hand. I awoke abruptly and sat up in bed. Later the next day, a phone called delivered the news that my nana had passed away.

During her life, my nana was a staunch Catholic who loved her masses and never missed one. She loved the dates November 1 for All Saints' Day and November 2 for All Souls' Day. I remember thinking how she would be pleased to know she shared that date with her beloved saints. My father made her final arrangements and set the date for her funeral: November 5, my birthday.

Shortly before her funeral, I bought an angel pin with rhinestone wings and topaz body, our birthstone. The angel pin was my gift to honor what we shared together and to protect and watch over her on the other side. At the wake, I asked the funeral director to place it on the lapel of her dress. At the end of the service, I stood in line with all of her family and friends to say goodbye.

I stood behind her two sisters, my great aunts, Irene and Emily. Irene was the middle daughter and a very tiny woman with a loud voice. Emily, the baby of my grandmother's family, was red-haired, freckled, and physically mirrored my Nana in body, voice, and mannerisms.

Irene leaned over my nana's body and began to weep in heavy sobs. As they walked her away, I struggled with my own emotions as I approached the casket. I leaned over her to say our final farewell and was startled to see a tear leave the corner of her left eye and run down her cheek. I stood in shock. Rationally, I knew it had to be Irene's tear, but it took my breath away. It looked as though my grandmother was shedding a tear between us as we said goodbye. I stopped and looked at her and the angel pin placed so neatly on her floral dress. The tear leaving the corner of her eye in perfect motion and rolling down the center of her cheek and down over her tiny chin.

I realized then that on that exact date 35 years earlier, my nana had peered into her newborn granddaughter's bassinet in the hospital and beamed. She was looking upon her future. She was beginning a new weave of unseen moments that would be sewn within her tapestry. And now, I was doing the reverse. I was looking at my past and knotting our final weave. There would be threads that surrounded her in my future, but none that would create living moments. Fate had made itself known through a date.

My threads with my nana had a predetermination to them, a defined beginning and end. Seeing this and understanding it makes the weave more profound and significant. Fate had played both a positive and negative connotation within our weave, but recognizing the connection helped me form a greater picture of our journey together.

The thread of intertwining fates creates a unique weave that is never apparent until the final result is displayed. The key to intertwining fates is to recognize the gift and accept that the moment was destined to be. Viewing the entire journey and being open to the thread allows us to enhance our belief in things bigger than ourselves.

There will always be threads that start from two different ends but are meant to intertwine in a precise, predestined moment. It is never apparent to those who are about to interact, but we must trust that the weave was always meant to blend together. Call it kismet or karma or fate, in the end what is destined to be will be.

THE THREADS OF TREASURE

"There's a treasure hidden in every moment, the joy of life is finding it."

~ *Katrina Mayer*

My husband was shopping on eBay one day when he found an old glass milk bottle from my father's hometown of East Providence, Rhode Island. I was getting ready to head out to a play at the local college with my mom when he called me over to look at the picture on the screen. It was just like the ones I remembered from my childhood. The sleek necked glass bottle with red lettering would have been filled with icy cold milk and my nana would have removed the cardboard milk cap before pouring it into my glass. My husband decided to bid on it as a gift for me.

"I hope you win," I said as I headed out to the car.

"Enjoy the play," he replied, eyes glued to the screen.

The play, *Life in a Glass Jar; The Irena Sendler Project*, is a story about a holocaust heroine who saved 2,500 Jewish children from the Warsaw Ghetto by recording each child's name on pieces of paper and placing them in a glass jar. The concept was one of hope of survival and reunion of the families torn apart by the horrible holocaust. And I'd heard good things about the production.

As I backed out of the driveway, my husband came out onto the front steps and gave me the thumbs up to show he had won the eBay auction and the bottle was mine. I was so thrilled to have a piece of history from my youth and could not wait to share the purchase with my mom.

Two hours later, seated in our seats near the stage, I noticed the glass jar they were using as the prop for the play. It was shaped just like the milk bottle my husband had won for me. I sat there in disbelief.

Many would have simply viewed that as a coincidence. But for me, there are no coincidences. There is only the opportunity for meaningful strands to touch mine and give me a message. In my mind, the glass bottle in the play represented hope for salvation and reunion. The milk bottle from East Providence meant precisely the same thing. My strand of the past, my salvation for the next life, and the hope for a chance to be reunited with my family again in my spiritual life. The strand floated by me like a cobweb, hoping that I would recognize and embrace it.

The irony of this day was in the meaning of the two milk bottles. One a gift of love that represented warm memories of my father and nana. Its sleek shape and bold red lettering brought forth nostalgic moments that epitomized a tether to my past and a hope of reuniting again. The glass bottle used in the play held its own magic of remembrance of all that was lost in the Holocaust and the hope that the slips of paper that held the names of the displaced family members would be able to rejoin again someday. The play was a depiction of complete and utter sacrifice in the times of a horrific war and the hope that emerged from the love of Irena Sendler. If you follow the story, the irony of the milk bottle is even greater in that a high school project in mid-America brought a woman from Poland to the attention of the world and showed how she overcame evil.

Three days later, the bottle was delivered and I proudly placed that East Providence 1950 glass milk bottle with my collection of vintage milk jugs. It sparked memories of sitting in my nana's kitchen eating homemade chocolate pudding and drinking an ice-cold glass of milk. It was as if that empty bottle was filled with happy memories and nostalgia for me.

Treasures are not just made of silver or gold. They are the threads of our lives and the people, places, and things that we valued most within it.

That is the beauty of really understanding the treasure thread. It is so multifaceted and has so many levels. When you take them all in at the same moment, the love and thankfulness you feel are immeasurable. Seek your treasure threads and take note of them so that when capturing the opportunity to revisit them the picture you see is as colorful as a kaleidoscope.

The treasure thread is not always apparent to the naked eye. It slides in and out of the picture in a camouflaged fashion with glints of vibrancy as it becomes part of the picture. It serves as a solid thread that is the basis of our dearest thoughts, beloved happenings, and people who have touched our lives.

Treasure threads are a constant weave within our tapestries, often sewing themselves into our foundation. They shimmer brightly when we recall, review, or reflect a portion of our life and see the moment with a new eye and the power of hindsight revealing all of the valuable facets, some we may not have appreciated at the time. The warmth, the emotion, and the intense longing of the event can reveal the gleam of a treasure thread and make it a lasting presence in our masterpiece.

THE THREADS OF PROJECTION

"Our minds influence the key activity of the brain, which then influences everything; perception, cognition, thoughts and feelings, personal relationships; they're all a projection of you."

~ *Deepak Chopra*

During significant periods of my life, there were times that it was apparent I was wallowing in self-doubt and what I perceived to be a failure. During these episodes of self-rejection, I was unknowingly projecting that image of myself to others. I cast this thread out to whoever came into my presence, always attracting the reactions and treatment that validated this thread.

It wasn't until I finally hit a personal low that I recognized the punishment I was inflicting upon myself. I watched friends and family achieve things I only dreamed of while I was steeped in resentment and envy. I lived in fear of disappointing or upsetting those around me and made it easy for people to put me last on the list. Time and time again I would hear the words, "I knew you would understand," or "I figured you wouldn't mind."

It was then that I decided to change how I saw myself. I was important and valuable. My feelings and opinions counted on every level and it was an honor to know me. I realized that I needed to start from within myself to project a different colored thread. I began telling myself this day in and day out while fighting the feeling that I sounded selfish or self-absorbed. I fearlessly rocked the boats of those around me and made it known that I would no longer tolerate mistreatment.

As I valued myself and re-created my projection thread, so did those around me who truly treasured me in their lives. They moved in-step with the dance and accepted the projection thread. Those who rejected it no longer held a place in my life. It was a difficult transition, but once I changed my internal thinking and became grateful for my gifts and embraced who I truly was, the weave made my tapestry even richer. Becoming aware of the message I was sending to others added a profound worth to the tapestry itself and set necessary boundaries. With this new mindset, I began to live a richer life, write a book, change a career, travel and no longer fear that I was not worthy of all of this before me. It was life-altering.

There are threads that originate from within which are exclusive of our own design. They connect and interact with other souls and tapestries around us. These threads can convey a tone or a persona of ourselves without us even being aware of the message. The demeanor of the thread cast dictates how the person will receive and respond to it. In other words, how you present yourself to others is exactly how it is received. If you feel guilty, it conveys to the person that way. If you feel confident about an idea, then that is how it will be perceived by others.

It is important to cast our threads in a way that positively projects what we want to convey. We must go deep within ourselves and try to envision how others see us. Being confident and true to our convictions is what makes our threads expand and reach all others in the best way possible. We expand our parameters of life and increase its quality.

Colors, textures, and dimensions are all a part of who we are and what we create in the grand scheme of things. Living our lives in a way that we wish to be perceived is the goal. We are remarkable and unique beings and should strive to leave a lasting picture of positivity and kindness.

THE THREADS OF A GRATEFUL SOUL
AND A THANKFUL HEART

"To speak gratitude is courteous and pleasant, to enact gratitude is generous and noble, but to live gratitude is to touch Heaven."

~ Johannes A. Gaertner

After I graduated from college, I tried so hard to find a job in my field, and although entry level for a woman at that time usually meant secretarial work, I had invested in an expensive education and wanted to attain an entry level management job. Finally, after a year of pounding the pavement and filling in with a temp agency to supplement my income, I found my entry-level job.

I remember that first day like it was yesterday. Typewriters dotted desks around the office. The clicking of the keys as they typed out memos and other correspondence was like music to my ears and I hoped it would forever remind me to be grateful for my start on the path of employment.

Years later, when my husband and I were first engaged, we went on endless house viewings in an effort to find our new home. I made a habit of driving through some of the local neighborhoods in the evenings to catch glimpses of families sitting around tables in their kitchens or gathered in front of the televisions in the living rooms. My heart would long for those moments and I couldn't wait for us to find a house of our own.

When we finally found and bought a house, on our first night there, I stood out front and looked in through the picture window from the road. I pretended I was driving by and imagined what our home looked like to others passing by. Moving forward, I made a point to ensure that not only did my home have curb appeal, but that it reflected a beauty of family and pride of home ownership. I wanted anyone passing by to see the gratefulness I felt for my beautiful home.

As the years passed, my job became stagnant and felt like drudgery and I longed for something new. My house began to age and I no longer saw its charm, rather I saw all the things that needed to be improved upon. I looked at them both with jaded eyes. The joy that had come from the job and house I had worked so hard to acquire lost its luster because I was no longer grateful for what they represented or thankful for what I had.

There are times when it becomes very difficult to wake up each day and appreciate all the wonderful things that surround us. It is too easy to become complacent and fill our lives with empty happiness that is created by the acquisition of material things. Jobs can start to feel more like an unsatisfying obligation and family dynamics may not be on the level of where we would like them.

The thankful heart, however, seeks to find true joy by seeing those same things in a positive light. But in the same way that you can't expect to get the toned muscles and cardio benefits without putting in the physical work at the gym, neither can you wake up grateful each day without taking the time to be thankful for all you have been given.

Experiencing the gifts of thankfulness and gratitude does not require you to have incredible wealth or an abundance of friends. It only demands that you take each day and find something unique and special within it. Be grateful for the ability to hear the birds sing or for the chance to talk to a loved one. Be thankful for the glorious wonder that is a sunrise or sunset, or for the sound of the pounding surf as the tide rolls in.

Gratefulness comes from a place of grace and its threads keep our tapestries' weave tight and strong. It is the acknowledgement of all of the things, little and big, and seeing them for the blessings they are. It is not seeing your dinner plate as half-empty or full, but instead recognizing that you are fortunate to have this food to eat and this plate to eat from. See the world through the eyes of honor and bounty. Grateful threads make moments feel richer and the people, places, and things in our lives more priceless. Sewing our tapestries with these threads lay a foundation of always seeing the world and everything in it as a blessing.

Greet each day with a heart that is thankful for all that is given and a soul that is grateful for the blessings and miracles that abound. Then imagine your tapestry's texture and hues. The colors of your lives can only be enhanced by this practice. The chromaticity will become so vibrant with gratitude that your tapestry will practically glitter with colors.

The regular habit of thankfulness is not as easy as it sounds to achieve and it requires a significant amount of practice and patience. There will be days when illness, loss, or ill fate will overtake your frame of mind. This is normal. What needs to occur is a mindset that says today I weave a positive picture because I am grateful for the food in my pantry, the family that surrounds me, the job that I have. So many simple aspects can change our otherwise negative outlooks. Weaving the colors and simple textures of thankfulness allows us to temper our negative feelings and base that day on a foundation of good.

THE THREADS OF SPACE AND TIME

"The secret of change is to focus all of your energy, not on fighting the old, but on building the new."

~ Dan Millman

When making the decision to write this book and share my ideas I never once considered myself to be an author. That term denoted a status that was too prestigious for me. Inside I wanted to share the concept of this book, but my inner voice would overpower my abilities and keep me from moving forward. I dabbled for years with the words and the paper and then realized the path I was on did not provide me with the growth I needed to take the next step. With fate placing opportunities on my path and my true self urging me to step out of my comfort zone, I began the journey forward to becoming an author.

Venturing into uncharted territory, I joined a writers' retreat and showed up at the old inn reserved for our event as a novice writer in a world of established authors. As part of the program, all of the writers had to pitch their books in front of the group. I quickly realized the difficulty in baring my soul idea, my words, and my abilities in front of a group of established writers who would critique my work. I listened as some of the other authors shared their ideas then stood to pitch my own.

And I bombed. Tanked. I had no idea what I had gotten myself into and sat down, deflated and insecure. The feedback, although encouraging, suggested that I change the basis of my book and alter the direction it was going.

By the time I went to bed that night, I knew what I had to do. I was going to excuse myself from the group, slip into the night, and leave my failure behind me. Since there was no cell phone service, I emailed my husband and mother at midnight to let them know I would be making my escape into the remote countryside of this mountain retreat at dawn. They both implored me to stick it out, but I had made my decision.

My alarm sounded at five a.m.; I dressed quickly and carried my packed bags out into the hall, ready to flee this debacle. The inn's old wooden stairs creaked as I made my way down to the landing. I tiptoed across the wide-planked wooden floor into the kitchen where I planned to make myself a cup of tea to go and leave a note detailing the terms of my surrender.

As I walked into the warm, homey kitchen, I heard a noise. There was no light, except for the soft natural light of sunrise that bathed the room in a dim glow. One of the other writers, a gentleman with his blue robe tied loosely around his waist, mussed hair, and grey slippers leaned against one of the kitchen's large windows, sipping his coffee.

There was no way he could have known of my plans to flee, but I swear he could read my intentions.

He hailed a "good morning" with a raise of his coffee mug.

"You know, I've been thinking about your book all night," he said, his voice low as he took another sip from his mug. "I can only imagine how hard it must have been to hear us tell you that you would have to rewrite the whole thing to make it work."

I stood there, my mind racing. 'Oh, my goodness,' I thought. 'He thinks I'm a loser and now he sees I am a quitter, too.'

Before I could say anything to defend myself, he told me how my book had touched him. "I fell asleep last night thinking about the threads of my life. I think you've got a great idea, you just need to give it a little punch."

As I stood there trying to take his words in, my inner voice, squawked in my ear, 'He's just being polite.'

Then he uttered five words that from that point forward changed my writing direction. "Go hard or go home."

He'd offered the mantra as a way to comfort and inspire me and I suddenly felt the urge to fight for this written creation of mine and see it through its journey. I couldn't help but wonder if he somehow knew I had come downstairs intending to run away or if he just had the uncanny ability to provide a fellow writer some sound advice just when she needed it most. Whatever his motivation, he convinced me to stay and rewrite my book. His challenge and his belief in my work were all I needed to change my direction.

I returned to my room, packed bags in hand, and began the arduous task of rewriting three chapters for the nightly pitch session. Needing to clear my mind first and shake off the funk of self-doubt, I pulled on my sneakers and went for a three mile run. I ran through a beautiful and remote mountaintop landscape that gave me the inspiration I needed to rewrite those chapters.

That second night's pitch, after much agonizing and restructuring, went so much better. I nervously presented my chapters to the group. During that presentation, those in the room were no longer the "more experienced" come to critique my work, but instead were simply my fellow writers, all of whom wanted me to succeed. I felt a surge of pride and accomplishment. When I had completed the pitch, some were in tears, but all received it with great accolades. The comment that "I had knocked it out of the park" gave me the "punch" I needed to follow my path and embrace the journey ahead.

This experience provided me with the chance to do something above and beyond the norm of my life. It expanded my confidence level and enhanced my tapestry with colors, textures, and a depth I had never expected. Had I just simply stayed within my safe zone and not taken a chance to put myself out there, I may not have ever experienced this level of self-awareness and pride.

When you begin to weave with your threads of space and time, remember to keep sacred the space of what once was while still leaving room for the weaves of what has not yet been designed. To envision the melding of these two spaces of time you need to be open to learning from previous weaves and trust that the key to a happy life is positive growth. Strengthening the good and trying not to repeat the negative is a crucial step in designing our tapestry.

THE THREADS OF SPIRITUALITY

"Everybody needs beauty as well as bread, places to play in and pray in, where nature may heal and cheer and give strength to body and soul alike."

~ *John Muir*

Shortly after the passing of a family member, the burdens of life that had touched our family began to take its toll and my husband and I found ourselves in need of a brief getaway. We needed a place to rest and rejuvenate. Miraculously, a kind friend offered us his timeshare in the Berkshires for a long weekend respite. We were thrilled by his kindness and gratefully accepted his gift.

It was the week after Christmas and the town of Lee and the old homes and business establishments were still beautifully decorated for the holiday. Every white, scalloped, picket fence was adorned with fresh evergreen swags, every light pole and front door with a wreath. The whole of Main Street was illuminated with twinkling lights and old-fashioned lanterns. It was like walking in a Currier and Ives picture come to life.

We spent our days touring several of the small towns in the area, shopping, antiquing, and experiencing the joys of fine dining.

On our second night, I experienced a restless sleep. I tossed and turned and entered a detailed dream world. I began to dream about hiking toward a high mountain. As I looked up the narrow gravelly pathway, bordered by tall lush green grasses to the peak of the mountain, I saw an angel sitting on the edge of a crag of rocks. He was seated on a ledge that jutted out over the edge of the slope, with his head down and his beautiful white wings wrapped around him. I could make out the large white feathers that engulfed his body and thick dark brown tresses of hair that covered his head. I was immediately drawn to him. I began my trek up the side of the steep cliffs walking faster and faster, keeping him within my view. As I walked higher and higher, I could look down at the valley below, but for all of my efforts, the angel remained the same distance away. I remembered grasping rocks in my hands to help pull me forward, but I could not reach him.

I stopped for a moment, standing very erect, peering up at him. He stood and looked down at me and opened his heavenly wings. The span of the white-feathered wings was enormous. He displayed his bare chest and I could see a gleaming heart with showers of light emanating from it. I caught a glimpse of his kind face. He smiled and began to fly away. And then I was standing in this enormous field of grass that stretched across the mountainous terrain, watching him fly away, and I felt so comforted. Just as I was embracing the moment, the dream faded away and I woke up.

Though I often shared my dreams with my husband, that morning, I was so emotionally touched by my dream that I decided to keep it to myself. I wanted the chance to really think about why I had dreamed about something so intense and try to discern its possible meaning.

With the angel's appearance still buzzing in my mind, my husband and I got dressed and went to find breakfast. We settled in a lovely café in the quaint town of Stockbridge. It had a very eclectic ambiance, including some morning entertainment in the form of a banjo-playing duo. At the end of each of the banjo necks was a wooden puppet that moved with each strum of the instrument and gave the impression of dancing. I was mesmerized by the sight as I sipped my latte and devoured a plate of cinnamon French toast.

When the musicians took a break, I finally told my husband of my dream and how comforted I felt and how I sensed that I had been in the presence of something truly miraculous. My dream recaps were a regular morning ritual and as usual, he listened to me with great interest.

As my husband got up to pay our bill, I remained at the table. I happened to look down at the seat next to me and noticed a colorful trifold map. It was the town map designed to show the hot spots for tourists. It was open to the first page and there, colorfully illustrated, was the hill from my dream. The brochure called it the Shrine of the Divine Mercies. I had never heard of the place, but I knew instantly that we needed to go there. I picked up the trifold map and showed it to my husband. Within minutes we were driving to the shrine.

As we approached the address indicated in the trifold, my breath caught in my throat. The drive up the gravel mountainous road past the descending hillside carpeted in tall grasses and statuesque pine trees was a mystical sight. In front of us was a large white statue of Jesus with a beautiful church behind it. The massive sculpture of Jesus welcoming all of those that followed that road was before me, beckoning me to follow. His arms were outstretched, with the sleeves of his robe draped out like angel wings, exposing his sacred heart- similar to the stance of the angel in my dream. I was so caught with emotion that I felt tears well up within me. It was as if my dream had come to life. I stood along the roadside and just stared at this miraculous form, taking it all in. It was an overcast day with a cold chill in the air, and yet in this place, I felt a warmth and contentment I had not felt in a long time. Large pine trees towered upward toward a stony grey sky and stood like pillars flanking this beautiful sight. A soft cool breeze wafted through this heavenly spot caressing my face and enlivening my soul. I felt as if I had entered hallowed ground in a divine realm.

As we finished our pilgrimage at this beautiful shrine, I decided to purchase a special memento in the shrine gift shop. I was drawn to a rosary bracelet with emerald beads and gold links that was displayed in a glass case. When I got to the register, the sweet young clerk behind the counter said I had picked a lovely bracelet. She said that it was made by a new supplier, based out of Providence, Rhode Island. I knew then that it was truly meant for me, for that place was where I was born and experienced my first spiritual connections. It was as if I had been called to this place, high above the town, looking down along the beautiful scenery below.

That magical adventure gave a charge to my spiritual self that had become depleted and unfulfilled. On that day, what emerged from my heart and soul was an energy of love, peace, and contentment.

Experiencing such an intense dream and then being able to experience it in my waking life was a spiritual calling. I was able to sit in the chapel and pray at the most beautiful of altars. I stood outside on a great platform built on the side of the hill, high above the town, among the tops of great pine trees, and embraced its sacred ambiance.

The thread of spirituality is different in each and everyone of us. We can seek and visualize divinity on so many distinctive levels. The importance of the thread is to connect to a higher power. When we allow our spiritual thread to be received then the gift of peace enters our tapestry. Our life is charged with a light and a pureness that cleanses our weave and allows our picture to span beyond this world.

Whenever I have inquired of those around me what they visualize within themselves, the terms spirituality and higher powers often populate the answers. It is met with different viewpoints, but often gives forth a feeling of harmony and a vision of pure light.

For me, angel wings, white feathers, butterflies, and rainbows elicit a higher power connection. When I see these things, I am immediately connected with the ethereal side and instantly feel comforted. It is important to have these reminders to align us to our spiritual mindfulness.

Encouraging the spirituality strand to grow and expand our weave gives strength to the foundation of our creations. It is important to seek out the mystical avenues that call to our hearts. These groundworks within our tapestry allow our minds to be enlightened and our hearts to be open and loving. It also provides us with the vision to see beyond this life and to seek a better path on our way to that place we hope to be eternal.

The beauty of the thread is that it can be shared and woven to many other strands within a large area. It has the capacity for great love and a great many connections to all living things. It allows us to be humbled by the presence of something greater than ourselves and can help us see the beauty and wonder that is around us every single day. Whether it is the majesty of a mountain, the depth and width of the great oceans, the infinite wonder of our skies, or the tiniest of flowers in bloom, we can see that there is more to life than just the threads that make up our souls. There is something else, something both internal and external. It is the most connected thread of our tapestry and the one that can comfort, enlighten, and mystify our lives with just a single stitch.

THE THREADS OF SUNRISES AND SUNSETS

"Rest but never quit. Even a sun has a sinking spell each evening. But it always rises the next morning. At sunrise, every soul is born again."

~ *Author Unknown*

I was marrying my college sweetheart. Our engagement announced, we set our wedding date in September. I embraced planning my wedding with joy and excitement, but I struggled to pick a song that my father and I would dance to at my wedding reception.

My mother had requested to not go the obvious route of "Daddy's Little Girl" because she felt it would be too emotional. My Dad and I had a favorite song together – Stevie Wonder's "My Cherie Amour." He had sung it to me countless times from the time I was a young girl. When I suggested that song to my father, he immediately kiboshed it.

"I can't dance to that song, Jude," he said with a defeated tone. "I just don't think I could get through the first couple of verses without breaking down."

We reminisced on how he would sing the main verses and I would belt out the chorus "La la la la la la, La la la la la la." We laughed, but I was suddenly struck with how weepy that song made me feel as well.

In the end, I chose the song "Sunrise Sunset" from the play *Fiddler on the Roof*. I was never so affected by the words as much as I loved the melody.

On the day of the wedding my father, who I had never seen cry in my life, was very emotional. I came out of our living room in my beautiful ivory wedding gown and I could see how much it affected him. I was the eldest of three girls and the first to be married and to leave my parents' home. As he walked down the aisle, he sobbed, stopping only after we had reached the altar. He removed my veil before handing me off to my husband-to-be.

At the reception, he and I were called to the dance floor for the father-daughter dance. He put out his hand for mine. His large, olive-skinned hands blanketed my white fingers and we began to dance.

"Is this the little girl I carried?" The first line of the song played over the speakers and my father collapsed on my shoulders, the curls of my hair covering his face and he cried uncontrollably.

In previous years, I would have been mortified by the spectacle we had made in front of our guests, but as I danced with him, the words finally began to take meaning for me too. The sunrise and the sunset of me being his little girl was forever changing at this moment. It didn't take long for my own tears to being to fall.

As the song continued, the poignant words marked that moment. My sunset had been completed as the girl in his house, and my sunrise was beginning as a married woman with my own home.

Sunrises and sunsets are the colors of our souls. They mark the beginning and end of each day. They are the starting color of our daily journey and how we embrace them enhances each and every hue of our tapestry.

Sunrises and sunsets are visual aspects of our picture that can be metaphorically painted in our own creation with the birth and death of a segment of life. It is an unparalleled blend of colors that remind us of the beauty of yesterday, the accomplishments of today, and the hope for tomorrow.

Life is very similar to that concept of the sunrise and sunset. It begins with endless possibilities and ends with the termination of that day's goals and dreams of what may be accomplished with the next sunrise. Each person is destined to view a set number of sunrises and sunsets. It is impossible to see them all, but when either can be witnessed, embrace and drink them in. Sunrises and sunsets should be experienced by all of the senses. Feel the warmth of the sun on your face, the breeze on your skin. Experience the smells and the sounds of that moment. They are a gift to your soul. They are meant to color your tapestry. Make sure to stop and take notice of them.

THE THREADS OF MOMENTS IN TIME

"Do you know how there are moments when the world moves so slowly you can feel your bones shifting, your mind tumbling? When you think that no matter what happens to you for the rest of your life, you will remember every last detail of that one minute forever?"

~ Jodi Picoult

My father battled cancer for the last five years of his life. During his illness, he had fought the different stages of cancer and there was a sense, in my mind, that he could beat anything. Upon leaving work early one summer's afternoon, I decided to surprise my Dad with a visit. He had been battling colon and now kidney cancer. The years had been filled with hope and despair for his health and I knew a visit would help to brighten his day. My dad was a true family man. He loved barbecues, Sunday dinners, and watching the Red Sox. He had a way of allowing his children to find their own way while always letting them know he had their back. I think he was always aware of my anxious tendencies and my struggles and he always seemed to nudge in a protective manner to get me where I needed to be.

It was a beautiful summer day in August. The sun was so bright and yellow, the sky so blue. As I approached the house I noticed my dad was alone in the backyard. He was sitting outside in his favorite tangerine-colored Adirondack chair. He waved me over.

"Jude," he said to greet me, a name that always touched my heart with happiness. His smile said he was glad to see me, but his eyes said something else entirely. Like a glimpse at the threads of despair, what I saw in his eyes that day is forever etched in my mind.

He had on khaki shorts and a white and blue checked button-down shirt. His grey hair was impeccable, as usual, despite having thinned from the chemo. He had just seeded a small patch of grass and sat watching the flow of water from a sprinkler, dance back and forth over the wet, muddied soil.

I considered the rainbow of chairs that flanked the brick patio and choosing the yellow one, I settled down to enjoy my time with him. We said our pleasantries and then sat for quite a while, saying nothing, just staring at the sprinkler as it vacillated back and forth, clicking with each change of direction. At that moment, there was no need for words. The sun was warm on our skins, the birds chirped and the bees buzzed. In the distance we could hear the hum of neighbors mowing their lawns. It was, in many ways, a perfect summer day.

And then it hit me. I knew what he knew. He would not see the fragile white grass seeds that sat atop the soil take root and regrow the following year.

He would not live long enough to see another summer.

The combination of colors, sounds, and feelings emanating from that space in time did not gel with that somber realization. It was a perfect summer day, set against the backdrop of that singular understanding, a moment frozen in time and permanently woven into our tapestries. When I envision that day within my tapestry, it is not an elaborate weave. There were no knots tied, no threads bound, just wisps of moments lightly touching each other, leaving a picture forever formed within my masterpiece.

Moments in time take the colors, the sounds, and the feelings that exist within them and form threads to meld themselves into that picture. These glints of time, these watercolor images, help stir our memory or bring us back to a place that touched us for good or for bad.

Multiple tapestries can share one specific event in time and are often bound and colored in a similar manner as the picture comes together. But for each person, the value and the memory can be significantly different. The perspective and meaning of that frozen memory is distinct and unique to the maker.

There are other moments that are only meant for the one who created it. When these moments occur, they are beautifully designed and artistically handcrafted, and are as unique as their creator. They are a fragile piece of workmanship. They can be pleasurable and they can have a significance to them that makes them invaluable. These moments are like ghostlike images within the masterpiece, and appear as if one was looking at an old movie within the stillness of the cloth. Look upon these threaded memories as they emerge, for they will often reflect or signify an important event or turning point in life.

THE THREADS CAST

"Sometimes, reaching out and taking someone's hand is the beginning of a journey. At other times, it is allowing another to take yours."

~ *Vera Nazarian*

In 2010, I reluctantly joined Facebook assuming I was selling my soul to the devil of social media by making it my new friend. As I began the process of timidly accepting the friend requests that were coming fast and furious, I began to dabble in the world of putting myself out there. This new world confounded me, and it took some time to learn how the whole "comment" thing worked. As I began to venture a "like" here and there, or drop an innocuous "good job" or "love your hair," I noticed a comment made by an old high school friend, Lisa, on a mutual friend's post. She friend requested me after seeing my comment and I happily accepted her friendship and went on with my business.

It was more than a day or two later that I happened to notice a simple pink heart placed on her status with the words "St. Jude." I stared at that little pink heart and could hardly believe it. I had just prayed to St. Jude that morning because my father was ill with cancer and about to go through a very serious surgery.

I took it as a sign and did something unbelievably out of character for me at the time—I sent her a private message. I typed out my message, explaining that I had just prayed to St. Jude and that he was my patron saint and I inquired what had led her to post the heart on her Facebook wall.

I was filled with trepidation as my finger hovered over my mouse, ready to click the send button. What if she thought I was strange? Or thought I was too nosy and didn't respond? What if she unfriended me and told the whole Facebook world I was a stalker? Clearly, if there was ever a time to report me to the Facebook police it would be for this random message.

But instinct and curiosity got the better of me and with a simple click, I sent the message out through the mystery of the internet and waited.

Lisa immediately wrote back, sharing that her father was dying of cancer and she was praying for strength and hope.

Our conversation continued both that day and for the weeks and months that followed. We spoke of our fathers' illnesses, about the suffering and hospice, about death and grief. We shared so much during that two-year span that followed that we became bonded in a way that could not have ever been foreseen.

The thread had been cast in the form of a pink heart and the name of a saint. Had she not cast it or had I not been willing to catch it, I would never have had the fulfilling days that marked the end of the journey I shared with my father. In retrospect, I never could have imagined that a person I knew only in casual passing would play such a key role in my future. The threads that are cast can not only help and heal us in the here and now, but can also become a lifeline that we connect to in our future.

In casting our threads, we are expanding and changing our picture's growth. We are taking a leap of faith and embracing our own uniqueness. In letting go of the fear that may prevent us from releasing our threads, we open our picture to endless possibilities.

Cast your threads out with the belief that what you put out will potentially come back to you in the future. Imagine that you are casting a fishing line out into the world, each one laced with the opportunity to connect with others in a positive way. Courage and strength are required, as is faith that the thread you project will be received and welcomed in the manner you hoped. With each hurl of your line, you are sharing your gifts of time and kindness. Not every cast will lead to a promising return, but for those that do, the threads of connection that follow will only strengthen and color your tapestry.

THE THREADS OF LIVING WITH REGRET

"One day, perhaps, you will see for yourself that regrets are as nothing. The value lies in how they are answered."

~ *Steven Erikson*

The last three months of my father's life proved exceptionally difficult. By that point, he was incredibly weak. Cancer had ravaged his once muscular and strong physique and left him a very frail and thin man. The original chemotherapy treatments had left their mark of neuropathy on his feet and hands. He struggled to walk and his steps were unsteady. He would shuffle along to keep his balance. His hands and extremities were always cold and he was often forced to wear gloves. Holding things were difficult for him as well. Many of those final days were spent transporting him back and forth to the hospital for treatments.

My mom, a tiny woman, could not take him to his treatments alone, so family members volunteered to go with her. I worked in a small office with limited time off. I opted to fulfill my obligations at the office rather than take the time, even once, to take my dad to chemo. Family members, including my own husband, took their turn taking him to the hospital and sitting with him during the long monotonous hours of treatment.

They were agonizing treatments; many times, my father was too weak to receive them and would get sick while at the facility. I listened to the details of those anguished visits, but did not try to clear my schedule or take unpaid leave for fear of potentially jeopardizing my job. After only three chemotherapy sessions, the decision was made to stop chemotherapy and accept hospice care. It is painful for me, even now, to think of those times and how I could have been with my father when he needed me most.

My one saving grace was that by the time hospice started, I stopped working to care for him. He had only days, six in total, but the guilt of choosing work over his treatments changed how I felt about the conflict my job presented. My father was leaving forever and I wanted to spend every moment I could with him. It took that one emotionally heavy event to make me realize I could no longer put my work duty before family obligations.

When I review that year, in particular the choices I made, a sharp, poignant clarity comes bounding into view. After my father passed and I returned to work, I realized that the office had not fallen apart or stopped working without me. It did inconvenience some and that was unfortunate, but inconvenience is quickly forgotten. Those final days I spent with my father will stay with me forever. This hard-learned lesson made it easier when a similar event entered my life. The next time, I was able to respond in a more appropriate fashion and chose, without regret, the obligation that had the most profound and moral impact on my life.

Regret is not unique to anyone. Upon reflecting on my most painful regrets, what comes to light is that they often stem from a misguided concept of duty. Reflection on these painful moments can almost bring us to our knees. It can force us to see the mistake in our minds, repeating over and over, until it can literally make us ill. Regrets are a learning experience, but if we continue to go back, we do our lives a disservice. Revisiting a misgiving repeatedly can diminish the sheen of our tapestry. The key to it is not to repeat it, but rather to learn from it and move on.

Regrets are a part of who we are. They forge through the tapestry in some of the ugliest of colors and threads. But with each stitch, we are forced to work through those painful experiences and hopefully find its lesson. It is the thread that reflects a learning curve, an opportunity to correct a wrong, readjust a path or form an acceptance of what we don't want to repeat.

The threads of regret mark a picture or design of our past in a way that makes us look back and wish for a different outcome. These dark strands often emerge throughout our lives, not just as a reminder of our past, but to coach us not to repeat that regret again.

Moving on and being able to see our regrets as teachable moments enhances our final picture. The pain it brings are reminders that we are alive, capable of redirecting our efforts and weaving the life we want for ourselves.

THE THREADS OF COMMITMENT

"My meaning simply is, that whatever I have tried to do in life, I have tried with all my heart to do it well; whatever I have devoted myself to, I have devoted myself to completely; that in great aims and in small, I have always been thoroughly in earnest."

~ *Charles Dickens*

When my father was in his final stages of cancer, we had a choice about the details of his care. We could place my dad in a facility where he could get around-the-clock care from a nursing staff or we could pursue the hospice at home with care provided by the family. It was a heavy-hearted decision with no positive end, but one that was a no-brainer. As a family, we were committed to seeing my father through to the end, even if it meant around-the-clock care. As we swore to a promise of letting his life end with dignity and love, we had no idea what we were marching into. We, my mother, sisters, husband, brothers-in-law and grandchildren, were cloaked with an armor of love as we waged a war with death.

As we sat with the hospice nurse who barked out commands as if we were an oncology surgical team, we all felt a commitment to see him through with as little pain as possible. She handed us a booklet on what to expect in the days to come. Inside, the clinical truths of what the body goes through as it prepares for death were revealed. My youngest sister and I looked at the booklet cover and laid it down on the coffee table. Neither of us was willing to anticipate my father's impending death as if he was just a body. We were told this could be as short as days or long as three weeks. Although neither sounded pleasant or fair. We could not imagine life without the man that was the glue of our little family. We faced challenges and medical issues during those days that were difficult to navigate, but with the help of the hospice nurse, we were able to effectively medicate my dad through the rough patches.

Our hospice nurse, a stocky woman with a stern face, had little warmth to her. She was almost unsympathetic to our plight and newness to this terrible domain. But what we learned through this brief relationship with her was that it was she who allowed us to hold it together and act like little soldiers furiously and tirelessly working through this land of death. Her tough-as-nails approach allowed us to be more fastidious in our duties rather than be the emotional wrecks we internally felt.

It took my youngest sister, Mary Beth, and I several days to drum up the courage to open the dreaded booklet and read the signs of death and learn how to prepare for those moments. After we read it, for some reason, it did not feel so evil or upsetting. We had just given our armor more strength.

Although my father was in hospice for only six days, it was an exhausting but peaceful journey. As the last day approached, and it was apparent that this was the end, my dad breathed his last amongst his wife and three daughters. It was what he wanted. He had asked us to do this and we gave him this gift.

My commitment to my mom and to our hospice nurse was to record the time of death. I remember feeling empty and numb at the time I had agreed to do it. It was almost like I had existed in that moment in time and agreed to something simply because it was asked, not because I really wanted to or even because I had needed to prevent that task from being passed to another.

As my younger sister and I recognized the change in breathing, and watched his chest rise for the last time, she looked at me and I at her. Then I turned and faced the clock. There was no repeat breath as I waited and waited, staring at my dad's alarm clock. Still holding his right hand in mine, I uttered out loud "time of death is 10:00 a.m."

It did not seem real, it was more like I was an extra on a movie set. But I discharged my duty with efficiency and commitment.

Moments stitched by the threads of commitment demonstrate who we really are, what we are capable of in our toughest times. The threads of commitment are there to show us that the obligations we have been put in charge of are ours alone. As hard as it may be to follow through, we emerge a better person because of the promise we make and keep to ourselves.

Normally, we surround ourselves with those who are akin to our own personal ethos and morals. We have similarities that keep us bound to each other. We often choose to pursue careers or live in places that also follow along those avenues. Marriage is another commitment that has such defined levels as the union is bound before family, friends, and God.

The threads of commitment are the threads that bind us to another. They are the promises that tether tapestries together. It is the intricate knot, tied with both the threads of love and commitment that binds a family, friendship, or business venture. It is the thread that sews our good name and ethical self to the thread of another.

When you enter into any commitment, remember to see the thread as it knots to your foundation as a representation of your true and good self. You want to have it reflect a beautiful picture of who you are and how you want to be seen by others now and in the future. When you become a person of integrity and good moral code, you want that persona to stand out and shine amongst the others. The knot that binds should be pure and strong.

Threads of commitment may not be easy to maintain, and they may not last forever, but the knot and the weave created at the time of commitment must reflect the just and kind person you are inside. These threads will resonate throughout the image and when viewed from any angle, will deepen the heart of the tapestry itself.

THE THREADS OF DIVINE
INTERVENTION

"Everyone sees the unseen in proportion to the clarity of his heart, and that depends upon how much he has polished it. Whoever has polished it more sees more – more unseen forms become manifest to him."

~ *Rumi*

One summer Friday night I found myself alone. My husband was in Vermont for the weekend fly fishing with his father. I had an urge to go have a bite to eat and get out of the house, but what to do? My youngest daughter, Catherine, was out with friends, so I reached out to my oldest daughter, Sarah. She was working as a bartender at a local restaurant and I texted her to see if it was crowded. She said it was very busy but to come anyway. It was a beautiful summer's night with a light warm breeze, blue sky, and what promised to be a spectacular sunset.

I texted back that I was on my way.

When I arrived at the bar, it was packed. I felt dismayed and uncomfortable and almost changed my mind about staying. At that moment, two gentlemen were paying their tab and they signaled me over to take one of their two bar stools. I thanked them and immediately sat and perused the menu.

It was loud and there was a lot of movement, but for some reason, I noticed a petite woman leaving the restaurant area. She was dressed in white, her straight, dark hair pulled back into a ponytail, a takeout container in her hand. The woman chatted with several people as she made her way through the crowd, and she walked up to the bar to say goodbye to my daughter.

She glanced at me. "Mind if I leave this here while I run to the ladies' room?" she asked, putting her takeout container on the empty stool beside me.

"Certainly," I replied with a smile.

She returned a few minutes later and sighed. "I don't want to go home, I wish I could stay a little longer."

I picked up the white takeout container and placed it on the bar, and tapped the top of the glossy wood stool.

"Have a seat. Relax and enjoy the view." I nodded toward the large bank of floor-to-ceiling windows that framed a view of the spectacular rolling green lawns that stretched out behind the club. Behind them stretched beautiful farmland and a glorious, soft pink sky.

She settled onto the stool and ordered a drink. "My daughter and grandchildren moved in with me not too long ago. I came out tonight because I needed a little space. I love them dearly, but I just wanted one night of not putting them all to bed. I just want to be Sophia tonight. Not Mom, Grandma, or wife. Just Sophia."

As we chatted, she shared that her mother-in-law was in hospice care and how hard it has been. She then shared how she felt about her own mother's recent death and being with her during her hospice care. My own father had recently passed and we settled into conversation, each perhaps unconsciously aware of the relief that came from being able to talk to someone else who knew how hard it was to care for a dying parent and how honored we were to be a part of their passing.

We discussed our experiences and how similar they were. Sophia had flown down to be with her mother in Florida for three weeks. Her mother had lamented to her that she felt terrible that Sophia had to leave her family and tend to her.

"I told her, 'Mom, I want to be with you and when you pass I will open a window to set your soul free.'"

This statement grabbed my attention and stopped me in my tracks.

I immediately explained that I too had opened a window in honor of my father's passing.

She looked at me just as shocked.

It always haunted me that my gesture, a simple opening of a window, could be construed as saying "Goodbye, see you on the other side," or that I was encouraging my father to "give up the fight," but I had done it as a sign of respect and love, a recognition and acceptance that he was spiritually free. I lamented that I would never know if he knew what I had done, or if it had even been the right thing to do.

I asked, "When did your mother pass?"

She replied, "January 20, 2014."

When she shared the date, it was like my heart skipped a beat. It was exactly a year to the day my father had passed. This perfect stranger had the exact same experience I had on the same day. We were in awe of our similar paths and how we ended up strangers in this place discussing our lives.

I knew that my desire to go out to eat, and the seemingly chance encounter with Sophia had all happened by design. It was all in response to my question. My father knew I opened the window for him. He, and possibly Sophia's mother, went to a lot of trouble to let us know that they were near and knew what we had done for them. The timing and the subject matter were too close to not believe a message was sent.

It was a gift from beyond the veil, a thread both Sophia and I were meant to share and validate together. It was a gift of spiritual openness. To miss that meaning, or to dismiss it as less than what it was, would have been tantamount to rejecting this benefaction. To repudiate the opportunity to see beyond the ordinary and not revel in the message would have been a shame. In the days, weeks, months, and even years after my father's death, so many of these kinds of threads were (and still are) cast to remind me that he was not entirely gone from my life.

On another occasion, my husband had to pick a company gift for the celebration of his 15 years of service. He perused the gift brochure, but could not find anything he liked and asked me to pick. At first, I said no because he had earned the reward, not me. He insisted and said time was running out. On the top of one of the pages was a beautiful marcasite bracelet in sterling silver. The jewelry company who made it was called Judith Jack. Its velvet case even had the name embossed in gold on the top.

I looked at my husband and asked, "Would you consider a beautiful bracelet for your years of service?"

He responded with a smile, nodded, and ordered the bracelet.

I wear it often and think of my dad each time.

Another time, on a trip to Costco, just weeks after my father's passing, I was feeling exceptionally melancholy. My father loved to shop at Costco and it reminded me of him so much that I sat in the parking lot feeling very grief stricken. Just then a large white pickup truck with lettering on the side that read in big black print JACK AND JUDY'S ANTIQUE RADIOS pulled into the spot beside me. I stared at the lettering and felt my spirit lift. Jack and Judy – my dad and me. Again, the thread was cast. The parking lot was huge and full, and yet the one space next to mine happened to bring forth a car with our names on it. I went into Costco much lighter and with a glowing sense of inner peace.

But perhaps one of my favorite divine threads was woven between my youngest daughter and me. For Mother's Day in 2016, Catherine decided to give me a very unique and beautiful gift. She commissioned an artist to craft a gold bracelet designed with my father's signature incorporated into the design. At first, she had struggled to find an example of his handwriting and signature. After going through many pictures and objects I owned, she finally discovered a high school picture with his name on the back. The beautifully written cursive signature inscribed in blue ink read... *Love Always, Jack.*

Catherine forwarded a picture of the writing to the artist. Because of the complexity of the signature, the artist needed a little longer than normal to complete it, but as Mother's Day was still many weeks away, my daughter was confident she'd found the perfect gift. The shipment confirmation she later received promised it would arrive in time.

But, the day before Mother's Day, the delivery had still not arrived. Catherine was heartbroken. She told me about her gift the next day, but feared it was lost. I was so touched by the thought and admired the picture and told her I would wait with patient anticipation for it to arrive.

My father's birthday was about a week later and he was on my mind. Alone in my house that evening, I was busy cleaning the kitchen after supper and the doorbell rang. When I opened the door, the UPS man handed me a tiny package. I signed for it and brought the little box into the living room. Inside was the precious gold bracelet. Its intricate design and delicate craftsmanship were breathtaking. But it was the words, now held in the palm of my hands that were so unbelievable. This tiny gold bracelet held the words written by my father so many years ago, before I was even a glint in his eyes, *Love Always, Jack.*

I called Catherine to thank her for my beautiful gift. She apologized for its late delivery. I assured her that it was not late at all but had come right on time. It came at a time when I needed to feel and hear from him most. The thread of divine intervention had touched my tapestry once again.

Do not close your mind to these moments, for they are meant to help us see what waits beyond us and confirm that we will all be together again. Threads of divine intervention are created and sent forth from another place in the cosmos. Many will miss these gifts merely because they do not believe or do not accept that there are opportunities to receive contact from those we are no longer able to see, those beyond the veil. But, to describe it as pure coincidence would be a disservice to the connection that was made. Threads of divine intervention are sent from beyond as messages of comfort and acknowledgment.

When these threads are cast into our dimension it is so important that we embrace them and allow the weave to enter our picture. They create invisible seams bound by love and faith. They are glittering segments that weave along the perimeter of our tapestry and allow us the opportunity to communicate and broaden our lives in a greater form. These wisps of threads, if heeded or accepted, make a shimmering non-color weave that reflects an ethereal light that enhances our final picture in a way greater than we could ever imagine. But if it is missed by logic and explanation, then that part of the tapestry remains stagnant, dulled by the lost opportunity for connection.

These divinations come in many forms. They can be simple reminders in the forms of a feather, butterfly, or penny. Other signs of contact can be sent through a familiar song, a recognizable scent, or electrical glitches like a light blinking or TV interruptions. There are anomalies that come at times to make us think our loved one is near.

Openness to these gifts is the only requirement for receipt of these connections. If one is open, the colors and textures of these unseen threads can enrich our lives so intensely that we cannot help but grow spiritually.

THE THREADS OF DREAMS

"I think we dream so we don't have to be apart so long. If we're in each other's dreams, we can play together all night."

~ *Bill Watterson*

My dreams are especially colorful and detailed. As I sleep, they will often address an issue I am afraid to deal with in my waking life or assist in working out a problem I may only be aware of in my subconscious state.

And still other times, I believe my dreams can be a tool for those family members who have passed to relay a message. In one of these dreams, for a reason I couldn't understand at the time, my father showed me his wallet. It was in the top drawer of his desk and I could see it so clearly, brown and worn. He would touch it with his long pointy index finger, then flip it open and tap it. It was a very simple dream, but I felt he was trying to show me something.

When I awoke, I called my mother and shared my dream with her. She told me that she no longer carried his wallet with her for fear of losing it and had no idea why he would be showing it to me.

Later that day, my mother was busy looking for a proof of payment for her gas company statement and she was unable to locate it. She scoured her usual places for documents with no success. It was then she opened a desk my father had used and there was his wallet neatly placed where she had left it. Underneath the billfold, she spied a folded piece of white paper. The gas receipt!

On another occasion I dreamed of my father's vintage house thermometer. It was about three inches high and three inches wide and made of brass and resembled a small clock from the sixties. For as long as I can remember, it was a treasured item of his. Shortly before he died, it fell off the shelf where he kept it and broke. My mother did not want him to know it had broken, so she had gently placed it back on the bookshelf until she could fix it.

In my dream, my father was pointing to his thermometer on the shelf and again using his long pointy finger, tapped it, and showed me how to repair it. He took the back of the thermometer and snapped it on to the crystal front. I could hear the click of the two pieces fit back together.

The next afternoon, I called my mother and shared my dream. To both of our astonishments, she told me how earlier that day, despite many previously failed attempts, she had decided to try and put the thermometer back together again. She described how she had brought all of the pieces to the kitchen table and tried to figure out how the pieces fit. The first attempt didn't work, but in her own words, as she tried again, the pieces clicked in place like it was made of magnets. She had felt as if she was receiving assistance from another while she worked on it. Restored to proper working order, she had placed the beloved thermometer back where it belonged.

My father, it would seem, recognized the ability for us to communicate in this dream state and it wasn't long before he reached out to me again. This time he showed me Nana's St. Jude statue. The stone-likeness had been a part of my grandmother's small garden for many years and when she passed away and my father sold the house, we all felt St. Jude should come home with us and be placed in his garden. It had taken up residence there, near his shed.

In addition to the statue, my father also showed me the St. Jude medal that hung on a gold chain from the mirror in his room. He was standing by the mirror using his hands and fidgeting with the medal that hung on the peg, running his fingers up and down the chain in a repetitive motion. I then heard the words in a muffled voice, "put that back." It was so loud and clear I awoke from my dream. Again, I shared my dream with my mom, but she had no idea what I was talking about.

"That medal hasn't hung from his mirror for many years," she said.

I assumed that dream had no merit and put it aside.

Weeks later while visiting my mom, we went to see the statue from my dream. It stood so proudly at the edge of a small perennial garden nestled between two tall orange lily plants. As I approached it, I noticed something shiny around its neck. I couldn't believe it. It was my father's St. Jude medal!

I turned to my mother in shock.

I exclaimed, "There is Dad's St. Jude medal from my dream!"

Shocked by my outburst she peered over at the statue. "Oh, I completely forgot we had hung that around St. Jude's neck shortly after your father took sick."

She shared that she and my nephew Jack, my father's namesake, were over by the statue and Jack went to remove the chain from around St. Jude and my mother uttered the words, "Please put that back!"

If I had to interpret what the last dream may have been it would be that my dad was letting us know he is with us in certain moments of our days.

After my dad died, those dreams were a turning point for me. It was as if he was trying to show us that he was still there beside us as we went about our day-to-day activities. The dreams were a salve for my grief and allowed my tapestry to brighten and grow. Allowing this thread into my picture has made my life so much more spiritually fulfilled.

Dreams can give us ideas and a purpose to strive for. They can occur both in sleep and awake moments and can provide us with the vision and direction to pursue goals that lead us to our destined paths. To be able to see our dreams as tools is a blessing. In everyday life, "dreaming" about an event or material object enhances our ability to make it happen. Whether it be a concrete design for a kitchen or garden, or an intangible spoken statement to express a wish or desire, dreaming makes the unreal come to life. The threads of dreams reach into our world from an ethereal plane and give our tapestry the ability to create and expand.

Dreams are given to us for a reason. They are the mind and soul's way of reaching new heights, facing fears we are not ready to confront in real life, or assisting us from becoming stagnant and fearful of change. To dream and learn from these creations only adds to our life's picture. It colors the tapestry with whimsy and weaves with rare and unique threads that are created specifically in the mind.

Do not be afraid to weave your tapestry with your visions. They are useful tools for solving issues, creating new paths, or even receiving comfort from those who are no longer with us.

THE THREADS OF CLARITY

"Brushing the clouds away from my eyes, I see clarity in the raindrop and beauty in the first ray of morning sun...Life is strange and wonderous..."

~ Virginia Alison

Every year, I devote an entire week of vacation to getting up early and running the Cliff Walk in Newport, Rhode Island at sunrise. Although it doesn't sound very restful, it is spiritually very fulfilling for me. I run solo, nothing around save a seagull or sandpiper. Every sound, smell, and sight registers in my psyche and for a short time I enjoy the luxury of forgetting about all of the things that weigh me down.

On one extremely grey morning, I rose quietly at dawn and grabbed the running gear that I had carefully laid out the night before. I dressed, tied my sneakers, banded my hair in a ponytail, and grabbed my phone and earbuds. Tiptoeing so as not to wake my husband, I exited our oceanside hotel room, and took the elevator down to the lobby, stretching as I descended. In the parking lot, I did a few more stretches before trotting across the street to the beach front. I was instantly met with the smell of the salty moist air and the sound of the crashing ocean waves.

Thick fog covered the beach, making the morning cool and dank and hiding all but the faintest of early morning light. I decided to jog the mile to the cliff walk entrance on the boardwalk that ran along Easton's

Beach. As I began my jog along the winding craggy walkway of the cliff walk, I peered out over the ocean. The massive stony-grey cloud cover that dominated the sky, opened for a minute allowing a beam of light to penetrate through and hit the grey-blue ocean below. The beam was a pure white tower of light and when it hit the top of the water it created a glowing circumference of illumination upon the ocean surface. It was so sudden and so impressive that I immediately stopped and snapped a picture with my cell phone.

It was a one-in-a-million moment and a chance-of-a-lifetime picture. Instead of thinking about my running time or the calories being burned, I walked. I stared at the heaven-sent sign for as long as it lasted, mesmerized by the powerful light against the dark. I realized that all of the things that fulfilled me – nature and God – were both present in that moment of solitude. I felt so connected with the beauty of our world. I was filled with love for the simple life I had, a life filled with kindness and generosity, and felt inspired to share my love with others.

My time spent on the Cliff Walk that day was entirely different than it had ever been before. I watched as the sun burned away the darkness of the clouds and how everything around me seemed to awaken. The butterflies flitted along the wildflowers that cascaded down the sides of the crags. The sparrows swirled about the brush and the sea ducks played within the shallows of the ocean below. I had been so accustomed to running through this area, that I had previously been oblivious to what was truly magical about it. Clarity at its finest, brought about by serendipity and serenity, had brought me peace and a new awareness of who I was.

Experiencing what fulfills our hearts and souls is the beauty of the threads of clarity. Seeing ourselves for who we really are and what makes us tick is not an easy endeavor. We are often muddled in the mundane and complacency of life. We become spouses, parents, co-workers, etc. and in existing in these variations of ourselves, we forget who we really are and what fulfills our being.

Finding a space and time where we clearly connect with who we are is the key to finding clarity. During these instances of reflection, we glean a glimpse into ourselves and view the picture we have created. We can touch the colors and hues and see the strength of our threads and the ties that bind to them. It is in these moments that we are able to enhance our tapestries by being able to validate its worth.

Threads

Allow yourself these occasions of quiet calm and reflection. Give yourself the gift of clarity and imagine all that has been created and all the colors that represent your life.

THE THREADS OF NATURE

"Nature always wears the colors of the spirit"
                    ~ Ralph Waldo Emerson

It was the beginning of May and nature was bestowing her bounty on the land. I was participating in a retreat that weekend and had left the world of chores, work, and other busy life moments behind for a couple of days. It was a gift to myself so that I could concentrate on my writing.

I sat on a porch in Vermont looking out over the mountainside and admiring an old white birch as it creaked and swayed in the wind. The leaves made a melodic rustling sound that swooshed back and forth in a wooden slumber song. A hummingbird darted above my head. I studied his feathers, his color, and shape of his body as I listened to the flutter and hum of his wings as he hovered near the feeder, sipping nectar through his long beak.

I looked out over the pond and instead of just seeing it, I really looked at it. I looked deep into the water as the breeze rippled the surface. I saw the clouds and distant mountain reflected in its glassy form. I looked beyond the pond to the endless fields of green covered with thousands of dandelions. I smiled to myself. At home, the dandelion is the enemy of every plush green lawn, but here it was practically revered as it formed a magical yellow carpet along the dirt road. The pine trees flanking the field danced in the wind, the green needles shushing the countryside and making the absence of man-made noise noticeable. I was completely enveloped in nature and felt so at peace. I completely let go of what the world had tied upon my mind. I found a freedom in my being that I had been missing. With that freedom came my writing muse and the level of meditation that made me feel complete.

When I returned home three days later, I was a whole person again. My family said I was energized and vibrant. This thread of nature made me realize how important it is to really escape the processed concrete world and return, even for an abbreviated time, to the natural world and recharge your tapestry. Let those threads stitch and meld into your basic picture and give rebirth and growth to your life. Visualize, open the mind, and see the natural beauty around you.

When given these moments of retreat, take in all of the sights, sounds and smells. See the trees, the blue sky, and the panoramic view. Feel the wind, hear the insects and the birds, discover every shade present in the blades of grass and other flora. Allow yourself to be taken in by the beauty. Give yourself over to it and recognize your place of belonging within that place. Feel blessed and be grateful that this is the world you were born into.

THE THREADS OF NEW EXPERIENCES

"The purpose of life is to live it, to taste experience to the utmost, to reach out eagerly and without fear for newer and richer experience."

~ Eleanor Roosevelt

While watching a television program one day, I sat transfixed by a woman talking about the extensive koi pond set up she had in her back yard. The pond was placed on the side of her house, just off the deck area. The layout was immense, but what captivated me the most was the golden retriever that sat at the edge of the deck, watching the koi. She would gently and quietly lower herself down to the side of the pond and the koi would rise up to touch her nose.

During this time of my life, my sweet golden retriever, Casey, was my constant shadow. He especially loved being outside with me while I worked in the gardens or he'd sit on my little deck area beside me as I rocked in my white wicker rocking chair. I knew if we had a garden area similar to the one I had seen on TV, he would love it. I imagined the scene in my yard, and contemplated where I would place the pond and how it would all be laid out.

As was often the case with many of the ideas I had, logistics, time, and money often rained on my parade. When we priced out my water garden, it soon became obvious that I was out of luck. Summer ebbed away, as did my idea and I was soon distracted by other things and moved on to other projects.

But the idea of a koi pond in my back yard was one destined to come to fruition.

It was the weekend of my birthday in early November and I was out running errands. On the way home, I happened to drive by a home having a tag sale. As I slowed my car to take a quick inventory of the items for sale, there it was! A koi pond system, filter, and materials. I immediately parked across the street and hurried over to talk to the owner. We shared our interest in water gardens and she had quite a bit of knowledge about the plant life and ecosystems required for such an endeavor.

I asked her why she was selling it and she explained she could never quite get it to take off and found the maintenance to be too much work. I could not believe my good fortune. We settled on $20 for the black, hot tub sized, molded pond form, the filter, bio balls, fountain, and large fishnet! I loaded it into my vehicle and drove home still hardly believing my luck.

I was beyond excited with my treasure, but it was too late in the season to even consider getting it started, so I reluctantly stored it away for the winter. While I waited for spring to return, I picked up books at my library and educated myself on the natural ecology required to sustain a water garden and pond. I mapped out where its location would be in our yard and made a list of the required landscape plants to place around it. I also read up on the type of fish that should be used. It all depended on the depth of my pond, filter size, and area climate.

When the spring season finally arrived, and the groundbreaking occurred, I was like a kid on Christmas morning. We placed the pond near the side of my deck, close enough to stand on the deck and see it, but far enough away to allow a walking path around the side of it. I added natural elements like large stones and picked a diverse variety of plants selected to make it look like the pond had always been here, including a colorful array of perennial plants to add some vibrancy to my water oasis.

Once the water garden was in working order, it was time to find my fish. I patiently waited for Mother's Day, knowing that was the key time of year to have fish outside in my location. I chose my koi based on color and size. Pretty soon the koi pond was bubbling and there was movement within its shallow water.

Years later there would be a magnolia tree that flanked one side and draped over the main pond, occasionally dropping luxurious pinkish white flowers onto its surface. Eventually we added a waterfall section, which would create more space and add the soothing sound of moving water to my little oasis. When the pond was in full bloom, with the water hyacinth, lilies, water papyrus, water Venus fly traps and reeds, the effect was dazzling. There were goldfish and butterfly koi, bullfrogs, and tadpoles. Butterflies flitted around the edges near the butterfly bush and bees buzzed along its outer banks taking sweet nectar from the various lilies that grew at the water's edge. Hummingbirds and dragonflies darted among the foliage making their gentle wistful noises. A flagstone walkway in deep hues of grey, plum, and blue encircled the pond and led to a beautifully arched arbor. A bird bath was added at the far corner just under the magnolia tree.

We had created our own little paradise, a little ecosystem unto itself all because of a TV show and a tag sale. And just like the dog on TV, my Casey would come out in the evening and sit by my side as I would rock and listen to the gurgle of the water splashing onto the rocks within the pond. He would make his way down the worn wooden stairs of my deck onto the flagstone path and edge himself among the flowers. He would lean his sweet gentle head over the water and nuzzle it like it was a toy. The largest of my old koi would surface, followed by two others, and touch Casey's nose. I would smile and take it all in. I had experienced my dream of living colors and textures. This new learning experience had enhanced my tapestry three-fold. I had created a little world of my own and I was grateful.

New experiences can be met with an array of threads and colors that meld together to create a section to our tapestry. We often meet new experiences with the exhilaration of excitement and a level of trepidation all rolled into one. Embracing these new experiences, and all those souls who touch your tapestry as a result, has an everlasting effect on the beauty of our lives.

There are individuals in life that close themselves to experiencing the world in a deeper and richer fashion. They choose to close their mind off from learning and experiencing things. To do this is to not allow their tapestry to grow to the capacity it was meant to be.

Should you find yourself hesitating to embrace a new experience, shut your eyes and think about how it would feel to commence the moment. Imagine the colors, the textures, and the length of the experience you could acquire. Envision the people you will meet and how their tapestries will accent your own. Grasp that opportunity to see new things through their threads and make the experience a growing one.

Take all of the experiences that come your way and immerse yourself in the learning process. Enrichment only makes your picture brighter and your journey sweeter.

THE THREADS OF THE WOVEN WORD

"Words have magic. Spells and curses. Some of them, the best of them, once said change everything."

~ *Nora Roberts*

When my youngest daughter was in high school she joined the cheer squad and became friends with Ashley and Evan, two very popular girls. Their personalities and social standings in the school were well known. Both girls were older, vivacious, and they embraced Catherine into their little group.

The girls were all slim with athletic bodies, dazzling smiles, and perfect features. When they walked into a room you could feel the charismatic pull of their bubbly personalities and beauty. One day, I found the three of them huddled together over my coffee table.

An array of school portraits was spread out in front of them in an organized fashion as the three girls began to systematically rate the best pictures for the yearbook.

"Mom, come help us. Which ones do you like the best?" Catherine asked with excitement.

Ashley, with her large dark brown eyes and glossy straight brunette hair, smiled at me nervously. I could tell that she felt a little intimidated by my assessment of their pictures. In my mind, I knew she needed a boost of confidence. Evan, on the other hand with her blue eyes, blonde hair and delicate features exuded such a high level of confidence that I assumed she was unaffected by my inspection of the photos.

As I poured over the pictures of both girls, I could not help but notice how every picture of Evan was stunning. Each shot was breathtaking. Her lightly curled blonde hair was expertly coiffed, her sparkling blue eyes bright and brilliant, and a set of beautiful white teeth emphasized every perfect smile. Even her outfit choices were stunning.

When I glanced up at her, ready to share my thoughts I caught a glimpse of uncertainty and insecurity. I was taken aback. How could this be? It was then that I realized, she was just as much in need of a compliment. She was no different than Ashley.

I stepped back and said how beautiful she looked and which ones I loved the most. I started to see her eyes smile.

Grabbing a picture of each girl, I placed them against our antique desk in our living room. I pretended I was Tara Banks from *America's Top Model* giving feedback on how marvelous each shot was. The girls giggled at my poor imitation of the stars on that show, but both girls beamed with delight.

Upon later reflection, I knew I made a difference to each of those girls in the delivery of my words and actions. I had recognized how much both of them had needed a boost, even though they showed it in dramatically different ways.

Tragically, two years later, Evan was killed in a car accident. It was a devastating event for all that knew her, but most of all her family and friends. It was only after her death that I learned that she suffered from the same level of insecurity that many of us feel. She had struggled with how she looked and had not seen the beauty the rest of us did. I was again thankful that I had taken the opportunity that day to tell her exactly how beautiful she was.

Every one of us carries a certain level of insecurity and uncertainty about ourselves and everyone has a story to tell. Life experiences, struggles, and common threads allow us to participate in multifaceted communications with each other. It is part of our human nature to look for ways to relate to the stories of others and communicate our sameness.

The words we carry with us and the way we convey them can make a lasting impact on our tapestry and the ones we touch. They can be gentle and nurture with softness of tone or they can crush and destroy

THE THREADS OF ACCEPTANCE

"Sometimes the darkest challenges, the most difficult lessons, hold the greatest gems of light."

~ *Barbara Marciniak*

When my daughter, Catherine, became ill with what was not yet diagnosed as her platelet disease, she was a junior in college and had to take a medical leave of absence. She had always been an exceptional student, very driven academically, and a perfectionist by nature. She had been encouraged by the school staff to take a medical leave of absence so that she could focus on receiving treatment while keeping her GPA intact and freezing the financial aid status that she had received for good academic standing.

Through the respite, she worked very hard to improve her health so that she would be able to return to school the following semester. She followed all of the necessary treatments her physicians required of her and studied dietary regiments that would help her body to recover. She also decided that during her time of hiatus, she would continue to study for the classes she was forced to put on hold so that when she returned she would be more than ready to tackle the academic course load.

I was her sounding board and her support mechanism. I organized her doctor appointments, played the role of driver, and was her all-around cheerleader so that she could focus on getting herself better physically and regain her life again. What we did not anticipate was that when it came time for her to return to school, she would have to be interviewed by the university psychologist and medical staff. Reinstatement would only be allowed if she completed and passed this assessment.

At first, I was surprised by this requirement, but then realized they were invested in her and her success. They needed to make sure she was both physically and mentally ready to return.

It was shortly after the Christmas holiday when the email to schedule the interview popped in my daughter's inbox. If all went well, she would enroll full time in the spring semester. As the scheduled date for the re-entry interview approached, my daughter and I both grew anxious about this process. What would happen if they deemed she wasn't ready? Would her goal of graduating be stalled, or worse, prevented?

She asked if I would accompany her to this meeting for moral support and I agreed. If nothing else I could be there to console her if it didn't work out as planned.

The morning of the interview was very cold and wintery though the sky was extremely blue and clear. The color of that sky marked our day with a visual of hope for the result we both longed for.

As my black Pathfinder roared along the 35 miles of ice-coated roads en route to the university, I could feel her anxiety growing. At first, we rode in silence, our thoughts battling with the radio for attention. Suddenly, halfway through our drive, she shut the radio off and for a moment all I could hear was the slosh of the snow under the tires and the whirring sound of the engine.

"Mom, I'm nervous that they will find a reason not to let me back into school this semester. I am afraid they will think it's too soon."

I didn't want to tell her, but I'd been thinking the same thing. I thought about how far she had come in the past six months and what she had been through. She had accepted it all with such maturity and grace. My mind rushed to think of a positive spin or downgrade my reaction to what she was facing ahead, but I knew that would be obvious.

Instead, I reminded her that she had acknowledged her illness with a strength and resilience that I had never witnessed in her before. "When the time comes, dig deep and tell them why this obstacle has made your education even more precious to you. Tell them what your goals and dreams are once you have your degree."

We arrived at our destination with minutes to spare and hurried into the office to check into the main hall.

"Ma'am do you drive a black Pathfinder?" the receptionist asked.

"Yes," I said, nodding my head.

"It's parked illegally. You need to move it immediately or campus police will issue a ticket."

My daughter looked at me, fear visible in her eyes.

"Don't worry, Cate. I'll hurry right back," I promised and raced out the front door and down the stairs, all the while scanning the frozen landscape. Snowdrifts and the monstrous piles left by the plow had reduced an ample parking lot to just a few cleared spaces. Finally, I spied it! A small, poorly plowed space, with a half-hidden *Visitor Parking* sign half buried in the snow in front of it.

I maneuvered my car across the parking lot and pulled into the spot. I hurried back up the stairs and stepped inside, thankful to leave the chilly wind outside, just as my daughter was being called in for her interview. Together, we walked side by side behind an administrator who led us down more than one long corridor and up several flights of stairs. My daughter and I didn't speak, and the administrator offered no words of encouragement or even any instructions. For the duration of our walk, the only sound was the squeaking of my wet Timberland boots on the freshly polished floors. I glanced over at my daughter, so petite and fragile. She was like Andromeda standing on that precarious outcropping, preparing to face the Kraken of re-entry into the college.

Having reached our destination, the administrator opened a door and waved us inside. The room beyond was long and narrow. At the far end, a slender man in his thirties sat behind a desk under a large wooden-paned window. He motioned to a pair of chairs across from where he sat and invited my daughter to sit. He politely asked me to sit on a couch closer to the center of the room.

As we took our seats, the acceptance thread wove at a mad pace between us. We had come to this place knowing that it was unavoidable and necessary. We understood the action had to be completed for her to continue her college path and prove she was ready, willing, and able to come back.

The school psychologist began his introductions and I watched as the wind blew against the window, temporarily whitening out the view with swirls of powdery snow. It was a mirror of the turmoil I felt going on inside the room.

The questions began, and my daughter answered, fielding them as if she was an expert. At one point, she was given room to speak freely and appeal her case. She did so, and brilliantly.

"This illness has brought a lot of change to my life, and some debilitating challenges," she began. She told him about the possibility of grand mal seizures, but also gave examples of how she could handle them. She shared some of the plans she had made and what this change in her life meant to her. With great candor, she explained how she was going to utilize this hardship and change her focus to help others.

"I have accepted my illness, the hardships it has caused, and the trials I must endure to realize my dream."

She continued with such force in her voice I was awestruck by her words.

"Acceptance of what has happened to me has made me realize how valuable my time and effort are in making an impact on my life."

The psychologist responded, "That is a very strong statement. You've been dealt a hard blow and it has made you wise beyond your years. Do you know what you want to do with your degree?"

"I want to make a difference in the lives of those who struggle with illness, mental illness, and substance abuse," she responded thoughtfully. "After going through my own health crisis, including depression, and coming out the other side stronger and healthier, I would like the opportunity to help others overcome their difficulties. I want those afflicted to see there is always a better way of life."

The school psychologist smiled. Teary eyed and with a voice thick with emotion he uttered, "Catherine, you are an impressive young lady."

He then turned to me and asked if I had anything to add.

I had agreed to come to be her support and if need be, add words to her defense. But at that moment, I was unable to speak. Instead, tears rolled down my cheeks in a rapid succession and I managed to share how proud I was of her. I had been so moved by her conviction and struggles that I had no choice but to finally allow a bit of the sadness that only comes with acceptance to seep into my heart. I had taken the assignment of her care like a soldier, not allowing the reality of her infirmity to touch my inner self. I could feel the knotting of my own acceptance threads in that moment. It was an anchor point that would allow me to move on in my life where I had previously stagnated and not realized it.

By accepting these threads into her picture, Catherine enriched her tapestry and was able to turn her original goal of psychology into something deeper. The entire process was wrought with anxiety and dread, and yet the outcome was far better than anything she could have imagined.

The threads of acceptance sprout from those moments when you no longer fight the inevitable, but rather choose to make lemonade out of lemons. Sometimes we are faced with an unpleasant task that we can't avoid. And no matter how hard we try to bypass this obstacle, in the end, we accept that we must do it. The trick is learning to climb over those obstacles in a fashion that will result in a positive outcome.

Accepting the life that is given to you and finding the gifts within that existence are rare and exquisite threads. When we put our minds to facing the challenges ahead and making the outcome of that struggle better than we anticipated, we make our own lives richer, our threads stronger.

The threads of acceptance often offer a sense of peace. They can dampen anxiety and despair so that calm and redirection can enter. Acceptance does not mean you don't improve your life or path. Goals are always important because they reflect a positive avenue of obtaining a greater self. Instead, this thread's true gift is that it allows you to see where you are and to be happy with the gifts around you as you work to achieve the life you want.

Acceptance can be one of the hardest threads to weave. To see it, we must be willing to relinquish control and simply enjoy the ride, see the sights, and embrace the invaluable lessons given to us by a dynamic life. Every moment of every single day, the earth moves and spins on its axis. The sun rises and sets in an ever-changing pattern. We are never in the same place in time or space again. Keep that in mind and accept the path you were given. Live in the moment of where you are, positive or negative. Remember nothing is perfect. Each tapestry has its own migration. The key is to accept what is and where you are and then work to improve upon the moments around you.

THE THREADS OF LOVING WHAT YOU HAVE

"How do we nurture the soul? By revering our own life. By learning to love it all, not only the joys and the victories, but also the pain and the struggles."

~ *Nathaniel Branden*

Inevitably, there will be times when we look at what we have and wish we had more. I have often felt the ache that comes from the desire for new things coupled with the inability to have them. A new car, a pool, and remodeled kitchen have all been on my wish list, and every time the potential to see them realized came into view, some other unseen expense would arise that would interfere with my desire and I would have to put it aside for a time. It was difficult, at times, not to feel envious as I witnessed friends and family experience some of the things I had wished for.

Then out of the blue one day, my daughter started to notice strange bruises appearing all over her body. She had been burning the candle at both ends with a heavy course load at college, finals, and work and we both figured she was suffering from anemia. I sent her to her primary care physician, thinking an iron pill prescription was in her future, but after her exam she was sent to the hospital and admitted. At the age of 23, she had been diagnosed with a serious, potentially life-threatening platelet disease. It was so out of left field that as it was happening, I remember feeling like I was watching from a place outside of my body, witnessing everything unfold as a quiet, unseen observer. As the days progressed into her illness, and I was forced to reckon with the seriousness of what was happening, I started to see that the cars, fancy appliances, and all of the items from my list were just stuff. They had no meaning, love, or warmth to them.

Soon after, I found myself consumed by efforts to understand her illness, the doctors, her care, and the potential of a lifetime of unfortunate side effects. I began to think of our visits to Newport that past summer, the car ride to Vermont to pick up our rescue dog Tobin, and the fun we'd had binge-watching Netflix episodes of *Gilmore Girls*. How I wanted to revisit those moments again and savor the simple joys we shared during those healthy days. In remembering those times, I wasn't thinking about the worn couch in my living room or dated countertop in my kitchen. I was thinking about the joy and the laughter. As I watched each drop of her IV treatments feed into her thin arm, I realized how precious my life was.

I looked around the room, the floor of the oncology ward and studied the families that were there. Many of us graced with hallowed eyes, a result of the worry and lack of sleep as we advocated for our loved ones. As I took it all in, what came into glaring clarity was the importance of the people in my life and the love we shared.

After that, I immersed myself in a life that fought very hard for my daughter and the care she should receive. When we had good days, we celebrated them in a richer and deeper fashion. We took day trips, went shopping, and ate at fun restaurants. When her platelets crashed and she had to be hospitalized, we ate popsicles together, ordered red velvet cake, and ate chocolate during her treatments. We binge-watched Netflix all night as the IV's dripped medicine into her frail body. We made the threads of those moments mean something. During those days, when my daughter's platelet count dropped to zero and the threat of hemorrhage and potential brain bleeds or strokes loomed large, I did not think of all of the material things I had or did not have. They didn't matter.

Understand that it is completely normal and human to want more and to sometimes struggle to keep up with today's definition of success. It's okay to want to go on nice trips, see wonderful things, and experience everything that this amazing world has to offer. But as we begin to want and acquire these things, it is vitally important to listen and heed those gentle reminders to appreciate and be thankful for what you have right now. It is an exercise that takes practice, and it must be consciously done, but in those moments of severe illness or as we face those unexpected trials, it will help us to stay focused on what is truly important to us.

In this world of bigger, better, and more, we can forget what it is like to have simple pleasures. My tapestry has been visited on several occasions by what I refer to as the little green thread called envy. The concept of owning something bigger and better is tempting at times and it is all too easy to get caught up in the drive to compete with one another.

It is in those "green" moments that I tend to pull on this important thread and reflect on what I currently have. I embrace the treasures of living beings that abound in my life and surround me with the richest gifts of all. I remove myself from all that is materialistically desired and relish the incredible gifts of family, friends, and shelter.

My life is far from perfect, but it is those flaws and imperfections that give the tapestry depth and character. I can want many material things, but none of that can truly lead me to the place my heart prefers to be. I have a lovely home. When I sit and write in my dining room in the early mornings, the sun shines in that room like it is an enchanted palace. My yard is a garden of wildlife and natural beauty. My pets, my beautiful furry soul-friends, surround me with their gentle sounds and companionship, my family's presence touches me throughout my day. When I focus on these things, I no longer feel like I don't have enough. My life, and the color of my tapestry, is composed of an eternal richness beyond material wealth or status.

Envision your world and what truly makes you happy. Wrap your mind into the colors and pictures that give you substance and feed your soul. These are the threads of loving what you have. It doesn't matter where you are in life, how much you have or how little. Recognize that all of the people you love and who love you are treasures to embrace. Honor them and make sure they know they are more valuable to you than any material thing. When you are with those you care most about, live in the moment and give of your time and energy. At the end of the day, and the end of your life, all of the material belongings are just things. Those with whom you have a connection are the treasures you will hold dear.

THE THREADS OF PAIN

*"It is our wounds that create in us a desire to reach for miracles.
The fulfillment of such miracles depends on whether we let our
wounds pull us down or lift us up towards our dreams."*

~ *Jocelyn Soriano*

One of the more significant and painful moments in facing Catherine's platelet disease diagnosis was when she had an appointment to discuss her long-term options with one of the doctors at the Dana Farber Cancer Institute. Although I had several medical issues that were physically very painful, nothing prepared me for the angst I felt for my daughter as we sat listening to the doctor share her prognosis. Words like "chronic" and "lifelong" hung heavy in the air and set the stage for a continuous and never-ending battle to be waged. It was not just the disease itself that was so frightening as much as the deadly effects that could arise if her body did not respond positively to her treatments. As I looked at her sunken frame, her sad eyes, and her frail white hands as they covered her face, I knew a pain like no other. Watching my child break down in despair at the delivery of a diagnosis from her doctor was beyond heart-wrenching.

I felt helpless. I knew that I would wage the war alongside her, be her advocate, and help her every step of the way. What I could not do was take her pain, her despair, or her reality away.

I wanted to tell her that she would still be able to have children someday, or that she would recover and be able to run another race with me again. I wanted to encourage her, wanted to tell her how I truly believed everything was going to be okay, but I wasn't the one whose body had, in her own words "betrayed her." I feared my words would only make it worse. A bitterness at my own inability to do anything more than just watch her suffer filled my heart with such an ache. At that moment, an overwhelming rush of pain surged inside me and made me physically ill.

I knew she had to fight it or surrender to it. But it would have to be her choice.

"Mom, I just need some time to think about everything."

It was understandable. Each of the treatment options offered to her required a major decision. I watched the light dim in her eyes. I heard the quiver in her voice. I felt the rigidity of her body in our embrace. Even within the weave of everything that had happened so far, that singular conversation laid a darkness and a coarseness to her tapestry and mine.

When she approached me a few days later, she had a new-found resolve to her voice. She had studied her disease and treatments and had begun to accept the monumental mountain she was going to have to climb. And she was ready to face it head-on.

I sensed her fortitude and a light grew between us. Catherine had emerged from that penetrating darkness with a strength I had not yet ever witnessed from her. Her stature began to lift and become stronger. Her eyes were fierce and determined. Her voice more sure and decisive. I watched her transform right in front of my eyes and felt my own body feeding off her positivity and resoluteness. It was as if her willingness to fight had morphed us both into warriors, ready to do battle with the unknown.

I can't say we would have ever asked for this pain or that the road we walked together was smooth and easy. It was marked with the promise of many hard days and nights ahead. I can attest to the fact that as we traveled through this painful experience together, we evolved into something neither of us could imagine. With each step, the threads of pain stitched rows full of fortitude and love. Along the way, we recognized all of the incredible people that had been placed on that road to help her. It has enriched our lives and bonded our family on a level we might not otherwise have ever achieved and that is forever a part of our lasting picture.

Pain, whether it be physical, emotional, or empathic, is a necessary evil for making us who we must become. No one ever wakes up in the morning and says, "Gee, I sure hope my day starts and ends with pain." It is not a feeling or emotion we readily choose. In fact, in most cases, we try to find the least painful way of doing anything that is presented to us. But, pain gives our tapestry the emotional depth needed to enhance our own hues and textures. The luster of pain threads vary in relation to the degree of the hurt. As the degree of pain grows, the threads become broad and deep, almost inky and slick.

If our tapestry is heavy with pain, it becomes void of all light. But as hope and strength enter into our lives, the texture begins to lighten and the threads themselves begin to pulse. Much like adding a pinch of salt to something sweet helps to enhance the flavor, pain allows the more positive emotions in our life to grow brighter.

And just as moments of happiness and joy color our tapestry with the most beautiful of hues, the darkness of pain pulls our essence into the fabric itself. Every tear shed, sob uttered, or moment of despair endured brings our tapestry to its most sacred core. For it is within these moments that faith emerges and the soul is fed with the realization that although our tapestry is unique to us, it belongs to a greater picture, a masterpiece crafted from that heavenly place.

I have had so many moments of utter pain. The usual suspects include death, rejection, alienation, illness, injury, and heartbreak. Most are too personal to put on paper, but all are uniquely mine. The reflections in these times have brought me to my most spiritual foundation. These occasions, so dark and difficult, have also brought the texture of my true faithful soul to bear. Knotted and coarse with battle scars as it may be, it is also victorious and stronger within its magnitude.

THE THREADS OF GOOD INTENTIONS

"It is only with the heart that one can see rightly, what is essential is invisible to the eye."

~ *Antoine de Saint-Exupéry*

In the days that followed my daughter being released from the hospital, Shari, an acquaintance of ours came by unexpectedly to drop off a gift. My mother was a regular patron at the local library where Shari worked, and Mom would often stop at Shari's desk to share concerns over my daughter's disease. Shari, in turn, would reach out through email to see how we were doing.

She is a beautiful woman in her early fifties with a gentle spirit and kind heart. Her nature is always quiet and unassuming. On the day she came to visit, I welcomed her into the house and we settled around the kitchen table. She opened the beautiful gift bag she'd brought and meticulously pulled out six medium-sized, smooth stones and put them on the kitchen table.

My daughter had been so sick and was exhausted from one of her treatments, and yet, she seemed to be so charged by this visit, intrigued by the unusual gift.

Shari held one of the stones in the palm of her hand, her long and slender fingers lightly caressing its surface as she described the mandala stones technique to us. She explained how therapeutic this medium was to help relax and calm the mind.

From inside the bag, she pulled an array of acrylic paints, a paint pallet, brushes, and gloss gel. We listened to her tutorial on how to paint the stones using smooth light strokes. In her description of our task, she mentioned that she thought this was something my daughter and I could do together while my daughter convalesced.

As we sat focused on learning this new technique, I watched my daughter's face soften and relax. Shari's beautiful smile and lovely blue eyes warmed my kitchen with such kindness that the nerves and concerns that had plagued me during that long week in the hospital ebbed away.

After about thirty minutes, she rose from the table and said she needed to get home to start dinner. She put her winter jacket on and wrapped her scarf loosely around her neck. Her blonde curly hair was neatly tucked under her black wool hat. She hugged us both and wished us well and just as quietly as she had entered my home, she exited.

I looked over at the beautiful gift and I was so touched by her good intentions. She had not only brought a material gift, but had left the gift of peace in my home, a level of namaste. Her actions were not necessary, but they came from a place of true kindness and love.

We now look at our finished mandala stones, touching them, feeling their smoothness and letting the peace emerge into our beings. Good intentions are just that- good. They enter our lives in uncorrupted weaves and keep the positive flowing through. Most of us will find that it is not hard to touch people with thoughts and actions of good intentions. Simple appreciation and acts of kindness are never without instant, positive acknowledgment. Such deeds are recorded in our tapestry, forever woven into the foundation of who we are.

There is an opportunity in every life to do good for others with no expectations of anything in return. Threads of good intentions are woven straight from the heart and reach out to bind with other tapestries in a pure, loving form. Threads of this magnitude are extremely rare and create beautifully crafted experiences that touch, tie, bind, and elicit a resilience of pure light. It is as powerful to the one being touched by these threads as it is to be the one who bestows them.

THE THREADS OF TIME

"The timelessness in you is aware of the life's timelessness. And knows that yesterday is but today's memory and tomorrow is today's dream."

~ *Khalil Gibran*

Looking back, there have been too many days in my life that begin with me racing the clock. Every morning, I hurried along trying to pack in as much housework and complete as many chores as I could before my 8:00 departure for work. Then I got in my car and raced through mild traffic to get to work and be at my desk half an hour later. My lunch break was another 30 minutes of rushing to make phone calls, picking up dry cleaning, and running countless little errands before hurrying back to work. After work, it was the same old thing. I hurried to the grocery store before hurrying home to make dinner, before cramming a workout at the gym into the last minutes of my day. It became a treadmill kind of existence. Dashing here and there and never realizing that life and time were slipping by me. I tied my sense of accomplishment and success to how much I could get done in a day.

The years flew and the first year at my job became my tenth in the blink of an eye. I witnessed the passage of time marked by my daughters' various stages of life. There were junior high swim meets, high school cheer competitions, Drivers Ed classes, college searches, and college graduations. The march went on and on.

I finally realized that there had to be something more than just the constant hurry and I decided to try to experience my life at a more tapered pace. I began meditating in the morning as I started my day and took time to sit outside on my little deck and appreciate the world that existed inside my koi pond. Instead of quickly throwing fish food at the surface of the water and zipping away, I lingered at the pond's edge and waited for the fish to surface. I was surprised to discover that I had more fish than I thought. New additions were being born right within this little mecca of life. I quietly observed the hierarchy of fish and watched how they interacted and ate and how many loved to play among the waterfall currents.

In these quiet moments, I began to be able to capture all of the things that I had missed as I hurried from one task to another. Time did not stand still when I stepped out onto the deck, but the quality of the moments improved. In these snippets of tranquility, I made a point to love and treasure all of the things around me. And in doing so, found a new love of self and a new appreciation of time.

Valuing time gave me the perspective I needed to take a leap of faith and follow my heart's pursuit and write this book. For this venture to happen, I would have to pull away from the routine and the hurried and measured-time parts of my life and set my feet on the path of creativity and awakening. I embraced the gift of time and of staying in the moment and took those first steps. Spending the minutes quietly loving my life and the things around me made it possible for my being to creatively share those things in my writings.

Time is that intangible thing that can never be stopped or frozen. It is the one thread that flows so quickly within our creation that it has woven large stretches of our picture before we even get a chance to appreciate the stitching. Time threads are sleek and fleeting. They whisk through our tapestry creating a momentum that is insignificant for our short-term existance, but becomes a very distinct pattern of stitching in the long term.

Life requires work, planning, and progression to keep in step with future growth. But it is the appreciation of time that makes our life invaluable. In doing so, time is temporarily halted, captured in the moments colored by the beauty and love that surrounds us.

Take the time to enjoy the view. Don't sweat the small stuff. Focus on what's important in life and try not to let time dictate the pace of the journey.

THE THREADS OF ADVENTURE

"Until you step into the unknown, you don't know what you're made of."

~ Roy T. Bennett

When I was in my early forties, I started the adventure of getting physically fit. I had always wanted to do a sprint triathlon, but didn't consider myself very athletic or able to effectively compete in one. I was overweight and out of shape, but I wanted to fulfill this bucket list moment.

I started running and walking long distances. I bought a bike and began training with a man who raced. He taught me how to maximize speed and longevity on the bike. I joined a gym and started to swim, increasing my laps until I was able to complete a mile in the pool in a single lap lane. With each small success toward my larger goal, the drive to put my body in one of the best physical shapes I have ever been in developed.

Although I was not overly fast or superb in any component, as a grouping I did very well. I had the vision of how it would feel to compete in a triathlon and how empowering the experience would be. I perused the area events and found an all-women sprint triathlon held in the eastern part of my state, about an hour and a half from my home. I loved the fact that the race supported breast cancer. At the time, I had two friends battling the disease. I paid my entrance fee and refocused on my training.

As the months drew closer, I trained daily, working with two coaches, who helped me with my endurance and speed on biking and swimming. I started the brick training, teaching my body to transition from one event to the other. My husband presented me with a beautiful triathlon suit on my birthday and the die was officially cast. I was going to be a triathlete!

In the week before the race, regret and fear kicked in. What the hell was I thinking? I don't want to be a triathlete! I don't want to swim in a lake with 1,500 women! What about all of those brain-eating amoebas that live in warm water lakes I had read about? My swim coach had assured me those were in the southern states, but do I really want to take that chance? I hate using port-a-potties! What if I have to use the bathroom after I come out of the swim? The transition time frame does not allow for that. How many times had I practiced running out of the water, changing into my bike shoes, wiping my body down, putting on my number belt, and grabbing my cap and my Burt's Bees lip balm? There was no time for a stop at the bathroom. What midlife insanity did I just sign up for?

Somehow I managed to keep my trepidations at bay and the morning of the race arrived. We had to leave the house at 3:45 a.m. to make the 6:30 a.m. registration and 7:25 a.m. entrance into the water. My husband and daughters rolled out of bed well before dawn and we loaded into my black Pathfinder, already packed with my gear and my bike attached to the rear rack. We began our drive on the Mass Turnpike in the darkness to my adventure. As we neared the race exit, tiny raindrops hit the windshield. Suddenly, long white, zig-zag bursts of lightning streaked across the black sky. Loud booms of thunder rumbled and shook our vehicle. What level of Armageddon had I sentenced myself to?

As we slowed and took the exit, we took our spot in a trail of cars a mile long, all headed to the race. In the darkness, red brake lights brightened and dimmed as we slowly moved forward, an entire caravan of competitors moving in tandem a few feet at a time. We were like lemmings following each other into the great unknown.

We pulled into the parking lot and found our spot. The dawn was in full form and the stony-grey clouds of that storm were moving away.

My girls opened their eyes and grunted. I got out of the car and quickly unloaded my gear to head over to the transition spot to place my bike, towel, bike shoes, sneakers, and basin for washing my feet. I had my supply of Cliff bars and energy gels, and my two water bottles were filled to the brim.

Competitors were placed into age categories and my age group had powder-blue bathing caps. The color uniformity was designed to help us know where to stand and what heat we were in. I waved to my family from my transition area and started the lonely trek to the beach to stand with all of the other triathletes.

The sand was a sea of blue caps, probably 500 in total. I wanted to stand with someone and find a companion to get me through this. But who? So many women had come together and were laughing and joking about our pending adventure. I opted to go and stand next to a woman who looked like me. She faced the water, but her body language said she was just as nervous as I was. I walked up to her to introduce myself.

She turned to me and said, "Judy?"

"Jeanne?" I replied in complete shock. Out of this entire group of triathletes, I had singled out a woman I had grown up with in my neighborhood back in Feeding Hills, MA!

That is the beauty of the adventure and the cosmos, you never know what surprise is waiting for you. It was her first triathlon too and there we were, two small-town girls from Western Mass., raised on the same dead-end street, standing on the same beach, wearing the same powder blue bathing caps, both preparing to go into the water at the same time. What are the chances! I suddenly felt very relaxed.

My swim coach warned me not to go out in front center, but to stay back a bit and to the side. She said I would be trampled less when the gun went off. The announcement came for us to enter the water. Jeanne and I looked at each other, victorious in our moment of impending glory, and wished each other luck. Idiotically, I forgot my coach's sage advice, and went out front and center. Then the gun went off and I found myself fighting for my life among all of the kicking feet and reaching elbows!

The arduous swim amongst the hundred other women in my heat was surreal. After my swim was completed, my body was beyond tired, but I pushed forward and ran to the transition area to find my bike. I wiped my body down, clipped myself into my bike shoes and off like a bullet I went! The jubilation was almost extinguished as I began the two-mile climb up a steep hill with my jelly legs, but when I reached the apex and soared down the other side, I had such exhilaration of joy in my heart. I WAS DOING IT! Twelve more miles to go! I had this! I could hear the cowbells ringing and could see my way to the transition area again.

On the side of the road I noticed two pretty, young ladies holding a sign that read "GO MOM." It was my daughters! They called out to me with words of encouragement. A rush of adrenaline coursed through my body. My girls were watching their mother follow her dreams and compete in her race.

When I reached the transition point, I jumped off my bike and slipped clumsily into my sneakers to begin the last leg of my journey, the run. My body had decided at this point that it did not want to continue. The promise of pizza and cake at the end of this arduous hell was no longer a great enough incentive to continue. I started to tire and began to walk and run in a rhythmic fashion. At long last, I entered the large finish area, and the cheers and screams of all those who had come to root for their family and friends gave me a boost to finish with gusto. I touched the finish pad with a mighty leap, heard my name called out on the loudspeaker and ran through a large green arch where two triathlon helpers were waiting. To my left was a water bottle, to my right, a medal on a green ribbon to hang around my neck! I had done it! I had completed my first sprint triathlon.

That day still rings so proudly in my mind. I did not win, but I did a damn good job. The best part of my finish was my family and friends standing on the other side beaming with pride. My adventure thread served me well for the next seven years as I competed in a total of four triathlons and countless road races, getting better and stronger in each. It gave me a sense of accomplishment and of pride and taught me that you are never too old to challenge yourself.

Adventure threads are a fantastic addition to everyone's tapestry because they encourage us to challenge ourselves to bring excitement and exhilaration to our lives while connecting with others who are experiencing the same thing.

The threads of adventure not only enliven our tapestry with movement, but adds a vibrancy of dimension in a rainbow of colors. They allow us to challenge ourselves physically, mentally, and spiritually and to step outside of our comfort zones. They encourage us to chase aspirations we know ourselves capable of without the fear of failure.

THE THREADS OF BEING GOOD TO YOURSELF

"Dare to love yourself as if you were a rainbow with gold at both ends."

~ *Aberjhani*

I am rarely sick and hardly ever call out of work. Taking time off and leaving my co-workers to carry the load of the office leaves me riddled with guilt. My criteria for calling out sick is equivalent to being on one's deathbed. In the past, sore throats, severe headaches, and colds were not valid criteria. Fevers, stomach flus, and even gallbladder attacks were only considered grounds for leaving early.

But one day I awoke too sick to go in. I was fevered, fatigued and achy, and every movement took tremendous effort. I decided to call into work, fighting through all of the regular waves of guilt and remorse. To my surprise, once the decision was made, my heart lightened.

I laid on my couch while my three cats ran about the house, chasing each other and running and sliding on a small area rug at the front door down the hall. I could not help but be amused and wonder which one of these nuts decided to create a luge out of my rug. How many times a day, while I was at work, did this mayhem go on about my house?

Maggie, our Golden/Great Pyrenees mix, was laying in the middle of the room with every toy she owned surrounding her as if it were a wagon train protecting its worth. She would open one eye and look across the room at the shenanigans and then go back to sleep as if the competitive slip and slide down the front hall was an everyday occurrence. Life, it would seem, went on in my house regardless of where I was.

I was just about to fall asleep when then the doorbell rang. Horrified, I went to the door and peered through the beveled glass design to see who was standing beyond the window, wondering if I should just send them away. I was a ghostly pale shade of white, dressed in a pair of polar bear fleece pajamas, and nowhere presentable enough to open the door.

A woman, dressed in a red cashmere coat and little navy-blue flats, stood on the front steps. I smiled when I realized who it was.

"Hi, Mom," I said as I opened the door.

"You stayed home today? You must be really sick."

I smirked as she came inside and handed me a freshly baked loaf of banana bread wrapped up in a plastic Ziplock baggie. She went into the kitchen and put on a pot of tea and I shuffled back to the couch.

We spent the afternoon nibbling on the banana bread, sipping our tea, and talking about life. I was feeling sick and my mom had come to take care of me. I felt so happy inside to have that feeling of being cared for like a kid again. What a treat for my mind and body.

The blank thread that had started my day had evolved into so many colors and textures in such a short amount of time. It was defined, not by the hours spent behind the desk at work with its mundane daily tasks, but instead by an adventure of healing and simplicity. Despite feeling poorly, I had been given the gift of a day with my mom. Totally unexpected and without a plan, my day had stitched a surprise in my tapestry filled with so many good feelings. I will continue to look back at that day as an accepted opportunity to be good to myself. And having recognized the courage it took to do so, the universe had sent me an even better gift—time with my mom.

There is another time that I can recall, when I accepted the opportunity to be good to myself. My girls were in school and I was home with a terrible head cold and sore throat. I laid on the couch that day with my black lab Corky. He was so happy to have me with him and our newly-adopted kitten, Valentine, came and cuddled with us both. I grabbed my camera and snapped a picture. It was a fabulous day of loving and resting. What I didn't know was a few days later my beautiful dog, Corky, would take very ill and would be gone twenty days later. I am eternally grateful that we had that day together with no interruptions.

Because I saw the thread as an opportunity to be good to myself, I was granted the gift of recharging my spirit and I benefited from the treasure it brought with it. This blank thread enhanced my tapestry in such great lengths but only because I chose to be good to myself first.

There are times in our lives where we simply can't perform our day to-day duties. We can become overwhelmed by the stresses that occur in our everyday lives and require a respite from the hustle and bustle of the world to mend and regroup our inner peace.

We have a tendency to not allow ourselves the time and space to heal our body, mind, or souls completely, but instead expend all of our energies on the outer world. Imagine this thread is put before you. It is composed of nothing, just a blank strand with no color. When you follow your inner voice and allow this thread to come forth, you also allow yourself the blessings you did not know were waiting for you.

Letting this thread in occasionally is essential to our health. Affording the time to be good to oneself does not just benefit us, but all those that love and care for us. It is within this weave that we are able to rejuvenate our lives and enhance our picture with a fresher and stronger image.

THE THREADS OF NEW SOULS

"I meet people and they become chapters in my stories."
~ Avijeet Das

Every June, for many years, I hosted a family tag sale at my house. My parents, sisters, and I would start the process of methodically going through our houses, looking for items we no longer wished to keep. We would pick our date and begin the tedious job of setting up tables in my garage and pricing our wares.

The humorous thing about our tag sales was that we would set up the night before and then walk around the tables in my two-car garage, scoping out potential buys from what the others had decided to sell.

My middle sister, Carol, never really had any junk, but rather items that she purchased and never used. Her table was the most popular. Next came my youngest sister, Mary Beth, who had practical things that she no longer had a use for but were only very gently used. My parents would offer up items that were valuable in quality and memories.

And then there was me.

My table was usually an array of things that were old and worn but that I did not have the heart to toss. My husband had a theory that the process of emptying shelves of items to list for sale was only an exercise to make room for the items we traded with each other on the night before.

During one particular tag sale, my mother affixed a white oval price tag marked ten cents to the handle of a worn, pale-pink colander and put it on their table to sell. It had been a gift received at her bridal shower and was the colander my family had used for our entire childhood. Years of use had left it a paler pink then when it started, but it was still sturdy and had perfectly placed slots for drainage.

I saw the pink colander, placed so stoically on the white card table surrounded by other household treasures. That colander had served my parents' home for over 35 years, straining the pasta we ate every Wednesday, draining our vegetables each night for dinner, and holding the quarts of strawberries that we picked on Father's Day each year for jams and strawberry pie.

As I began to walk around the table, I felt the urge to purchase it and place it in my kitchen. In turn, I noticed my sisters doing the same thing. We silently stalked around the table, looking at the colander, none of us making the gesture to buy, but each of us hoping someone would. My parents were completely oblivious to the silent ado this little kitchen item was causing.

As the day wore on and many of our items were sold, the colander remained on the table. I had made a silent agreement with myself that if it was there by the end of the day, I would ask to purchase it from my parents. It was just about time to close our tag sale when a sweet young couple with a baby walked into our garage. They were just starting out and trying to get things for their apartment and began picking through the things we had left.

My parents were beyond thrilled to meet this little family and so pleased that they were purchasing many of their things. Just then, the young woman, baby flanked under one of her arms and nestled on her right hip, picked up the colander and showed it to her husband.

My heart dropped.

She went to place it back down and then said to her husband how much she loved it and wanted it for her kitchen. He smiled and gave a nod.

I knew the colander was theirs.

My parents happily gave them everything they'd picked out and wished them well at the start of their life together.

"I thought you were going to buy it," my younger sister said sadly as we watched the little family walk down my driveway towards their car, treasures in hand.

"I thought *you* were going to buy it," I replied. But as their car pulled away from the curb, I suddenly felt so good inside.

The colander was going to be the same for this little family as it was for ours. Our threads had finished with this item and now they mingled for just a bit with these new souls and together we had a momentary bind in tapestries. For the briefest span of time, that family had touched our hearts despite having had no idea that a little ten cent item had such value in memories and traditions.

When we embrace the fact that at any time of our lives a new soul can emerge and make an impact on our lives, we also allow ourselves the chance to grow and live more fully. It is a soul's duty to touch and impact, in a most positive way, as many other lives as possible.

I prefer to think of the meeting of new souls as an honor. Sometimes the meetings are obvious and planned. They fit into the path we are currently on and enhance the journey. Others have a more spontaneous greeting and change life in the most profound ways. Whether they are people or animals, they all have an impact on our picture.

Animals possess a soul that can bring much joy and life to our tapestry. If all humans allowed themselves to see the world through an animal's eyes, they would see helplessness, innocence, and, above all, a piece of God. Animals are colors in our tapestries, they are unique souls that bring brilliance and levity to our masterpiece. My animals have all come to me in unique ways and I feel that each one was sent as a gift.

New friendships and acquaintances also enrich our tapestries. Being open to the differences of others and the knowledge and views they bring to your life can only help you grow.

Encompass the new souls that enter your life. They come in different forms and even the negative ones have a purpose. A smile from a stranger as they pass by can color our strands with peaceful and pleasant hues. These hues create a burst of colors that others feel as they pass by, therefore, binding a positive light at that moment to multiple tapestries. The negative encounters, although unpleasant, and sometimes damaging, can turn our lives on to another path. Those paths are the cords that bind our tapestries' dimensions. Regardless of the way we greet the new souls in our lives, they are miracles that can influence our world and enhance our lives.

THE THREADS OF BEAUTY OF THE BEHOLDER

"People often say that 'beauty is in the eye of the beholder,' and I say that the most liberating thing about beauty is realizing that you are the beholder. This empowers us to find beauty in places where others have not dared to look, including inside ourselves."

~ Salma Hayek

I once heard a story about a recently married young couple, neither the bride nor groom more than 18 years of age. They were married by a clerk at their city hall in a very modest wedding. The bride wore a simple white sundress with a pink sash tied around her slim waist and a pair of sandals on her feet. Her blonde hair flowed around her shoulders and she held a small bouquet of baby's breath, lily of the valley, and a few purple violets. The groom wore a crisp, white, button-down shirt and navy-blue dress pants. The couple was ecstatic over their nuptials and celebrated their marriage in a joyful fashion. Their wedding vows said, and their nuptial kiss completed, the bride's father-in-law took the young couple across the street to a little strip of quaint shops. He walked them over to a very nice shop with a fancy window display and pointed out the beautiful décor within its showcase.

"You may pick anything out of that window as your wedding gift from me," the father said proudly.

The young man, so handsome and so in love with his beautiful bride, smiled and said to her, "You pick what you would like."

She smiled as if so humbled and awestruck by the generous offer. "I know what I would pick."

The young man beamed and questioned his sweet young bride, "What?"

She pointed to a framed picture within the showcase. It was a crushed velvet picture of the Last Supper. The frame was intricate and heavy, but the picture itself teetered on the side of cheap or tacky. She looked up so innocently at both men and her eyes sparkled, "I think it is so beautiful, and something I would never have thought I would own."

The father-in-law beamed and the threesome entered the store to purchase the gift.

The bride's sincere appreciation for the gift and her love of it brought the story a unique blend of sweetness. When I heard the story, I instantly felt compassion for the young bride and her appreciation of something that had probably been dismissed by many others. It made me appreciate that beauty is truly in the eye of the beholder and should always be welcomed and appreciated.

There is a thread that is created for every one of us that grasps a beauty that is completely for our own eyes and hearts. It does not matter how anyone else views that beauty, the one that beholds that sight makes it completely true.

This story resonates for many reasons. It is so deeply touching because within this magical moment of marriage this family found beauty and meaning in something that many others would never have given a second thought.

How many times have we decided that an idea or an item was unworthy of our interest simply because it wasn't something we would ever have entertained as having value. Threads of beauty are uniquely individual. They reflect what we possess inside of us and should never be criticized or dismissed as ugly. There are many levels of beauty. Some of the most beautiful people in the world present with a homely appearance. Their beauty emanates from the inside. What a dull world it would be if all of the world's beauty was only the shallow layer visible on the outside of people and things. Being open to the threads of the beauty of the beholder gives us a chance to see things we might not otherwise ever have considered worthy of our attention.

THE THREADS OF LOVE

"Love recognizes no barriers. It jumps hurdles, leaps fences,
penetrates walls to arrive at its destination full of hope."

~ *Maya Angelou*

An elderly couple were frequent visitors to the doctor's office where I worked for many years. They were in their mid-sixties when I first started assisting them. The gentleman was very tall, about 6'3" and in very good physical shape. He had dark brown eyes and was fair skinned with thinning white hair. She was on the shorter side, stocky with a ruddy complexion. She had sweet, vibrant blue eyes and a very warm smile. They were a very gentle couple and would quietly come to my window, the woman first, and check in. She would offer the insurance cards and confirm the information for them both. They would sign their paperwork together and she would joke with him that she would pay his insurance co-pay, but he would have to buy her lunch. He would smile in such a way that I could tell it was the same way he'd done so when he'd first seen her many years ago. They would finish their business at the window with me and then turn to sit, side-by-side, in two chairs in our waiting room.

There they would softly converse while waiting to be called in for their exams. When the doctor came to take them back, the husband would motion for his wife to go in first. "Beauty before age," he would say as she entered the exam room.

Year after year they would repeat this ritual. But as the years continued, she became more withdrawn and he would assume a more active role during their visits. They still smiled at each other and joked the same jokes, but the gentleman was much more involved and began to do more of the talking. He began handling all of the business at the window, while she stood at his side, her eyes distant and blank. Her eyes did not shine in the same manner as they had before, but her smile was just as warm. The gentleman would bring her to my window and show her where to sign her name, repeating the date for each page, and then gently took her arm and led her to the same two chairs they always sat in. They would discuss their daily agendas, but it was the man who did all of the talking. His wife would just sit and smile while staring blankly across the room.

He no longer let her go into the exam room by herself, and would escort her down the hall into the room. Her visits became more frequent and he would hold her hand, always talking sweetly to her as if she still held the same conversations with him. He never once lost his patience with her or gave her any indication that she was not the same woman he had loved for all of those years. In fact, in my eyes, his threads of love had increased to a level of immeasurable and intense love for his wife. His devotion was no longer a connection of deep physical attraction or intense intellectual talks, but of a genuine adoration of a partner and friend that had forever bonded them as one soul.

I reveled in their fidelity and the fact that they truly and deeply loved and respected one another enough to see the other to the end. She still adored him and would beam at him with her beautiful smile, childlike now, but still warm and loving. Even in my limited interaction with them, I watched their love transform. There was a bittersweet beauty in their dedication to one another.

The threads of love have a uniqueness to them because they are not just woven into our own picture. They are the threads that span and knot and weave to so many other tapestries in our lifetime. They are the threads that create the vastness of our masterpiece and elicit a life force and luster to every tapestry it touches. The depth of our love and the extent of our love is often depicted in the picture we create. The amount of souls we allow our heart to regard only widens our tapestry and allows it to span to other areas. The weave that is created when the thread of love is involved is as intricate and as delicate as ever a thread can be sewn. The edges and the depth of the weave are so detailed and eternally bound that when the weave is broken or stunted, the tapestry itself seems to lose luster in those areas.

The threads of love are always colorful and warm and often shimmer with a glistening light. When the love grows, so does the length, hue, and texture. But if broken or withered, the result can be very dark and knotted. When you allow yourself to love unconditionally, you reap the benefit of a tapestry that is as vast as the lives it touches and the light it creates. Allow your tapestry to grow in love and you not only enhance your life but all of those around you.

THE THREADS OF TIMES PAST

"Time flies over us, but leaves its shadow behind."

~ Nathaniel Hawthorne

A few years back, my family decided to take me to the Berkshires to shop, dine, and peruse old antique stores for my birthday. My children, though grown and living on their own, had dedicated the day to spending time with my husband and me.

After several hours of shopping, we went into one of my favorite antique shops in the town of Lee, Massachusetts. It was a consignment shop of different vendors and hosted an eclectic variety of things. After perusing one area of this shop, I rummaged through their collection of old post cards. I had previously purchased some Christmas and New Year's postcards from the early 1900's from the same vendor and hoped I could find some for Thanksgiving since my birthday was in November.

I love to find postcards with the original postmark on them and actual writings from the sender. It gives a snippet of what life was like back in that time and how innocent the correspondence was. I found two adorable 1920's postcards for Thanksgiving. I showed them to my oldest daughter, Sarah, and was about to walk to the register when I noticed one that wasn't holiday related but had a beautiful saying on it. It had a picture of an old New England style village and white steepled church on it with a rainbow that spanned over a green hill. The postcard had a lovely poem written on it that struck my fancy and I just could not put it down. The poem read, *"How oft as children we did try, to find the pot of gold; That rests beneath the rainbow tips, and doth such treasures hold."* I instantly wanted it but knew it was more expensive than the other two combined.

I flipped over the back to read what the sender had to say and admired the old cursive style writing. There was a lovely note about the writer asking the recipient to come for a visit and that they had recently gone into Kennebunkport, Maine to purchase a horse. I then read the postmark of the card. It read November 5, 1913, postmarked at 3:30 p.m. I checked my watch and couldn't help but smile. It was 3:35 p.m. on November 5, 2016. One hundred and three years to almost the moment since the card had been postmarked!

When time reaches out to you at a moment like that you can't help but be in awe of how vast our tapestries really are and how far the weaves that connect us can extend. Mrs. Ansel Whicker was the recipient of this postcard 103 years earlier, yet for that brief moment in time, the past entered into my present and gave me a fabulous gift. My family rejoiced with me in my find and, once purchased, it permanently marked the wonderful day we had together.

Being open to the span of space and time and how it may touch you is a weave that enhances how our tapestries can reach another. When you open your eyes to a past outside of your own personal past, you start to see how small and precious our world really is.

The thread of times past is unique and we only rarely have the opportunity to have it woven into our tapestries. Only the extremely fortunate are able to witness the timeless texture of the strand. The connection of two threads from two totally different time frames, decades, or eras is almost mystical. The gift of the legacy is the wonder of this weave.

Think of receiving an object or picture from a distant relative. You have no knowledge of them in your current life, but upon learning more about them, you realize you have much more in common. It is looking at an old photo for the first time and connecting to that person behind those eyes or clothes. It is the melding of tapestries at two totally different time frames, but forever connecting the two lives, one alive and breathing, the other captured in the stillness of a picture.

Whether it be through genealogy or the finding of an old relic, when your tapestry touches the threads of times past, you begin to see how short your time on this planet really is. These threads give value to our present and in valuing these connections we can often gain clarity for our future.

THE THREADS OF THE CHILD WITHIN YOU

"If wrinkles must be written upon our brows, let them not be written upon the heart. The spirit should never grow old."

~ *James A. Garfield*

For nearly a decade during our annual vacation in Newport, Rhode Island, two elderly women came to the same beach we frequented, always at exactly the same time each day.

They would approach the beach path with deliberate and careful steps, lightly conversing with each other as they made their way out onto the sand. If I had to guess, I'd say they were in their seventies when I first took notice of them. On more than one occasion, I had thought about going down and talking to them, but I always felt as though I would be an intruder into their secret world. I never learned if they were siblings or friends, for they always kept to themselves and never engaged with anyone else on the beach.

The two women were similar in stature and build, with tanned, jiggly skin and always wore black bathing suits with baggy white shorts and matching, white, rubberized bathing caps. They walked slightly bent forward as they inched their way to their favorite spot several yards from the water's edge carrying a blanket, two beige towels, and two white Styrofoam boogie boards.

Having set up their simple, cream-colored cotton blanket on the sand, the two would head out to the crashing waves in tandem, boogie boards in hand. I'd watch as they waded out into the cool surf on fragile legs. Knee-deep in the ocean, they would Velcro the tethers around their wrists, pulling the white boogie boards behind them like some kind of fantastical ocean creature on a leash. Then, as if partners in a synchronized swimming exhibition, they would dunk, float, and swim.

As a physically fit woman in my forties, I could not take my eyes off of them. It was a marvel to watch the transformation of their elderly bodies into youthful play. I was astonished by these two wonders and their zest for life. I imagined that the magical salt water made their landlubber bodies weightless and the cold salty sea mist on their faces would enliven their color.

Even from the beach I could see their smiles and catch hints of their laughter as they began the ritual of boogie boarding back and forth on the incoming waves. It was as if for those 45 minutes each day, the water possessed medicinal qualities and became a veritable fountain of youth. Then as magically as it began, it would end. Like the stroke of midnight ending Cinderella's date with the Prince and turning her coach back into a pumpkin, the two returned to their original forms on the beach. They would cautiously edge themselves onto the shore from the breaking surf, pausing for a few minutes at the water's fringe to let the seafoam caress their ankles and the sun to warm their faces. Then, in unison, these two land-dwelling mermaids would begin the slow trek up to their blanket where they'd sit and remove their bathing caps, once again accepting and resuming the age of their bodies, despite their youthful spirits.

In the summer of 2016, we made our usual trek to the beach at Newport, but the two women who had helped me realize the importance of a youthful spirit did not make an appearance. I wondered if they were simply no longer able to fight the reality of time, or if one had been called home. Or if they had simply found another beach, somewhere warmer, that allowed them to continue their youthful play. I missed seeing them and made a mental note not to forget their zest for life in their favorite playground.

Possessing a childlike quality allows us to keep our tapestries youthful and our souls playful. In life, there is always time for acting mature, making sound judgments, and being responsible. But how many times has the smell or memory of our youth filled us with such beautiful sentiments that we want to go back and experience those moments again? Those joyful memories lighten our soul. That is what it is like to allow childlike moments to enter our hearts.

There are so many ways to enhance the youthfulness of our tapestries. Do something that makes your heart soar. Ride a bike, run in the rain, paint a picture, pick flowers, go fishing, body surf at the beach, or blow bubbles! Participate in something that makes your heart feel young. When you allow the child within you to blossom again, you find that your words become kinder. Your demeanor changes so that you are able to see the world with a sense of wonder, honesty, and newness.

The child within you possesses the ability to see everything and every day with new eyes. It is a quality that must be used carefully so that the people you encounter still take you seriously. The key is to find that fine line where you can accept the responsibilities that come with adulthood while still embracing the joy of life and of being young at heart.

When a little one enters a room, you feel their youthful energy. That is the thread of the child within you. These threads are always light and wispy. They are new and vibrant. They elicit an eternal light of openness and excitement. While these threads don't typically connect our tapestry to those of others, envisioning these threads and experiencing them on any level enhances our tapestry's depth and allows it to pulse with a fresher more vibrant mix of colors and textures.

THE THREADS OF REMINDERS

"Thankfulness is the beginning of gratitude. Gratitude is the completion of thankfulness. Thankfulness may consist merely of words. Gratitude is shown in acts."

~ Henri Frederic Amiel

One day, a large box was delivered to my house. Just the sound of the doorbell ringing and the postman standing on the other side of my glass door brought a cheer to my heart. As I took the box from him, I peered over at the address label and instantly saw it was for me.

I carried the box inside and placed it gently on the dining room table, then looked at the name of the sender. It was from my friend, Vickie, in Georgia. What a thrill to receive something unexpected in the mail and even more so for it to be a gift from a friend.

Inside the cardboard box was another box, and inside that box was something wrapped in bubble wrap. I slowly peeled the wrap away exposing the most exquisite ginger jar inside. The white jar had a lid on top with a diamond shaped knob, "a bit of bling," I thought with surprise. The bold, black words written in cursive on the front of the jar read: *Blessing Jar.*

I lifted the lid and inside was a silver mesh bag tied with a satin black ribbon. I pulled the bag out from the belly of the jar and saw it was filled with little embossed cards. A pamphlet inside the mesh bag called them "gratitude cards." The instructions were simple: anytime I felt thankful or grateful for something or someone, I was to write it on one of the cards. Then, when I had a day when I did not feel very thankful or was upset, I was to go to my Blessing Jar and randomly remove one of the cards and read what I had previously written. It would be a reminder that I am loved and very fortunate in my life.

How perfectly simple and powerful at the same time.

I placed the jar on my bedroom bureau and pulled out my first gratitude card. On it, I wrote: "On this day, 6/14/15, I feel grateful for my friend Vickie and the wonderful gift of the blessing jar."

I called Vickie later that day and thanked her for the gift and told her how much it meant to me.

Vickie's kind gesture spurred me to return the favor. She is a court reporter and works on closed captioning for the deaf and I wanted to find something of meaning for her. She has a true love of Helen Keller and Anne Sullivan and a vintage, early-1900's cartoon on the story and life of Helen Keller was available on eBay. With the bid won, the vintage cartoon was sent to her with much love. She told me she proudly keeps it in her office as a reminder of what she strives for and is grateful for it every day.

Sometimes, we can get so involved in our day-to-day lives that we can forget all of the wonderful things this life has to offer that are worth celebrating. We settle into everyday ruts and fall into traps that keep us feeling depressed or unhappy with ourselves. Thankfully, even if we do forget from time to time, the threads of reminders won't disappear. Instead, they lay dormant in our tapestry waiting for us to notice them again.

Although my jar is exquisite, the idea of a Blessings Jar is something anyone could create with the materials they have around them. It could contain pictures, the written thoughts of times cherished, or even objects that would remind them of something treasured. It isn't so much the fancy jar that gives life to the threads of reminders. In fact, the jar could be a shoebox or even a desk drawer. It is, instead, the conscious reminder to stay focused on what is truly important in our lives.

The extremely delicate reminder threads help us appreciate the gifts that have been bestowed upon us. They reflect and shine with what our hearts hold dear. They are composed of the lightest wisps of time and places that are often tucked away from our view for much of our lives. But, if we remind ourselves every single day to look for the incredible gifts that are around us, we can start to weave a picture that glistens and captures the miracles of those gifts. Once acknowledged, they are forever etched in our hearts and stitched in our beautiful tapestries.

THE THREADS OF FRIENDSHIPS

"Each friend represents a world in us, a world possibly not born until they arrive, and it is only by this meeting that a new world is born."

~ Anaïs Nin

One of my dearest friendships came from a relationship I formed in the sixth grade. Julie and I were two awkward middle schoolers with aspirations, dreams, and hopeless crushes on several boys. The usual span of giggles, teenage angst, and drama colored the initial years of our friendship with magic. We went through junior high and high school together, our looks and appearances changing over time, as did our taste in music and boys, and our interest in education and athletics. In the full bloom of our relationship, we learned to drive and started part-time jobs and spent endless hours on the phone commiserating over our latest heartache or pop quiz.

After graduation, I helped Julie move across the state and into her freshman dorm. I waved goodbye fully convinced that we would be as inseparable as we had always been.

But inevitably, the demands of college, newly formed friendships, and the fact that we were chasing different dreams saw our friendship evolve once more. Graduation came and jobs started. Before I knew it, I was engaged to my husband, bought a house, started my career, and began having children. And Julie was living in an apartment outside of

Boston having begun her career in a very prestigious law firm downtown.

Although we spoke several times a year and sent the obligatory birthday and Christmas cards, the friendship became a thinning strand within our tapestries, waiting for the chance to blossom again. Then it happened. The contact was completely lost and I could not reach her. She no longer had the same address, phone number, or email address. Our lives had completely changed, and the friendship halted.

A decade went by and I was standing in line at our local bank, waiting to make a deposit. The line was long ahead of me and behind me. Behind me, a woman sneezed. I turned to say "God Bless you" and I found myself staring into the face of a former high school classmate of mine and Julie's college roommate! We started chatting and she disclosed that she had recently re-connected with Julie and had her new email address. She wrote it on the back of a bank deposit slip and handed it to me as we parted at the bank counter.

I folded it and put it in my purse. Then, as was the norm, my life grew busy with the demands of teenagers and my full-time job.

A few days later, I had an evening to myself and decided to send Julie an email. I typed in the email address and stared at the subject line. What would I say? Would she know who I was by the email address? Should I even bother? Then I typed: "Hello, long lost friend. This is Judy." I wrote a short message about reaching out and where my life was now. I re-read it and then pressed the send button.

To my utter delight, the next morning, her response popped up in my inbox! We began to slowly rekindle our friendship with an email relationship over a period of months. Then we made plans to meet at her seaside home and see each other in person.

A decade has passed since that first email and we still talk every month. We see each other on our birthdays and have a girls' weekend every July. Julie is a beautiful woman with a successful career and an incredible home by the ocean. We spend our annual weekend as if we were sixth graders listening to music from our past and reminiscing and sharing new experiences as well.

It's almost funny to think how something as random as a sneeze breathed new life into our friendship. Julie and I are lifelong friends who enjoy each other's company. With our friendship, we embrace each other with a deep bond forged through the test of time. Our tapestry has now regained its friendship weave with a richer and stronger thread. These threads are the gifts that need to be nurtured and tended to.

On our last weekend get together, we sat out on a blanket on the beach watching the sunset on Plum Island. As we watched the slit of light sink below the horizon, we sipped wine and toasted each other.

Julie raised her glass. "We were separated for a while, but Jude, you are stuck with me to the end."

With that, I raised my glass, smiling at the sound as our glasses clinked together. "Amen."

If color and texture are given to our tapestry from the friendships we make, we would see a vivid array of hues and strength to the thread.

Friendships are the jewels and the precious metals that add the living pulse to our tapestries. The smiles received when we see our friends bring forth warmth and vivacious energy to our picture. Long-lasting and true friendships are rare and create the gold and silver threads. They are strong and resilient, but understated. When the threads are woven to one another, the image formed as the tapestries merge is pure magic.

Friendships of all kinds, whether they are life-long friends or short-term acquaintances, bring color and life to our tapestry. Each meeting helps us to grow and has a purpose. Even a negative kinship can enrich our tapestry in one form or another.

Always try to remember that every encounter with another human being is a chance to enhance your tapestry and help you grow in life.

THE THREADS OF CONNECTIONS

"Invisible threads are the strongest ties."

~ *Friedrich Nietzsche*

Every year my friend Julie and I take a trip to the North Shore of Massachusetts. It is a chance to let loose and for that entire weekend be the young school girls we once were. We spend a day on the northern tip of Plum Island, sunning ourselves, taking walks, and collecting driftwood. We eat out, shop, and usually try to do something special each visit. On one stay we decided to drive into Salem for the day and have some fun shopping and sightseeing. For our special thing to do, Julie booked psychic readings with a woman who lived near the pier. I was so excited to have my fortune read and to see what mysterious words from beyond she had to impart to me.

We spent the morning walking the cobblestone streets, taking in the sights, and shopping at the area stores. We found a quaint little café and sat outside for lunch, admiring the wharf. It was late July and cooler than usual for that time of year. The wharf was buzzing with tourists and the sky was a beautiful blue, dappled with stony colored clouds that played hide and seek with the sun.

On our way to the reading, we walked past the little harbor on to Pickering Wharf, and followed the directions to the door of the psychic medium's building. A short walk later, we stopped in front of a two-story building with stores on the first level. A single red door, leading to places unknown, stood between the two storefronts.

My stomach lurched a bit. Suddenly I did not want to do this. I looked at my sweet friend Julie and her blue eyes twinkled.

"Ready, Jude?" she coaxed.

I nodded nervously and knocked on the door, lightly at first, then a little harder. I could hear someone shuffling downstairs from within the townhouse. I waited and then the door handle began to turn, and the door creaked open.

Before us, in the dimly lit foyer, stood a tiny, older woman. She was just barely five feet tall and probably weighed all of 80 pounds. She had on a flowy white gauze shirt, open in the front to reveal glimpses of a petal pink tee. Her pants were white linen and she had on mule slippers adorned with rhinestones and feathers. Her hair was a yellow blonde with long wisps around her head. She was an attractive woman with a welcoming smile.

Julie seemed unaffected by this little vision and promised to be back in the half hour for her turn. I, however, was suddenly a little nervous about this strange tiny woman. After all, I had seen enough horror movies in my life to know I might not come back the same. I might return as a zombie or possessed by a wayward spirit.

The woman welcomed me into the foyer and asked me to follow her up the red-carpeted stairs. I quickly glanced around, making note of any possible escape routes in the event I needed a quick getaway from my little bewitching medium. At the top landing there was another door, white and modern. As she opened this door, the most beautiful natural light bathed the room. Inside was an incredibly posh living space with large windows that looked out over the Salem harbor. There was a fireplace adorned with beautiful figurines and an incredible painting of a ship hanging above the mantle. The floors were bare hardwood, except for a white fluffy rug in the center that held a circular rattan and canvas coffee table. There were books everywhere. The room was so lovely and warm that I immediately felt at ease.

"Psychic readings have been very good to her," I mused to myself.

In that instant, the psychic cocked her head and smirked.

"Great, she can read minds too!" I whispered under my breath, now even more unsure of what was about to happen.

She motioned me toward two beautiful chairs next to a table that was nestled in the corner. A deep purple, silk scarf adorned with gold crescent moons had been strategically placed on the tabletop. Its diamond shape covered most of the surface, but allowed the natural wood edges of the table to show. On top of the scarf was a deck of tarot cards, a yellow legal pad, and a pen.

She asked me to sit, relax, not cross my legs or arms, to allow her to read me. I sat quietly, but couldn't help but take in the marvel that was the rest of the room.

In the opposite corner, below one of the windows, was a doll-sized brass canopy bed adorned in plush white bedding and pink satin pillows. Inside was a tiny Yorkshire terrier with a pink rhinestone-covered collar and a pink bow in the tuft of the top of her head. On the bed beside her was a small white china plate, filled with lobster meat.

I could not contain my shock and disbelief. The psychic followed my surprised look and suddenly became defensive. She whipped her little head at me and snarled, "My dog likes lobster meat! Now be still, so I can continue to read you."

Despite my curiosity, I got through that part of my reading and we continued with the tarot card cutting and reading. First she gave me some financial advice. My husband and I were contemplating a financial deal that had me very uneasy but that he was more than enthusiastic about. She lectured me to allow him to pursue this idea since he was on the right track. I made a mental note to rethink my position on the matter, still not entirely convinced the investment was a good idea. But then she revealed some insight that proved life-changing.

"You are very creative and you have an idea that needs to be pulled from the universe and completed. Do you write?" she asked me pointedly.

As fate would have it, I had begun to dabble again in my writing and was currently writing what would become the first few chapters of this book. I hesitated to answer her question, but then I realized she was very serious. She was adamant that this held the key to my future goals and that success was imminent with this endeavor. "Don't delay. You need to get it done," she stressed.

As crazy and as comical as this meeting had been, tiny lobster-eating dogs and all, her advice that day cemented my ideas of creating the book *Threads*. The two solid bits of information she gave me that day panned out. As it turns out, the financial advice she gave me proved 100% correct, and her connection with me spurred my need to follow a path I had stepped on from time to time, without any real conviction until that day. This mysterious woman, who I had connected to for just 30 paid minutes, forever changed the direction of my path. Her insight led me to pursue something that was just under the surface of my consciousness. She did not add depth to my tapestry, or color, but in the making of that connection, my path was altered on to a more solid road.

In every meeting, a similar chance for our paths to be redirected exists. Whether the meeting be positive or negative, with an old friend or a complete stranger, there is a learned experience that comes with it and a chance to enhance our lives and make them fuller.

Threads from these encounters don't always add to the substance of our tapestry directly, but instead can enhance its growth substantially. They are meant to act as guideposts in our lives and point us toward the endless possibilities that exist if only we accept that they can be.

THE THREADS OF KINDRED SPIRITS

"Throughout this journey of life we meet many people along the way. Each one has a purpose in our life. No one we meet is ever a coincidence."

~ *Mimi Novic*

My parents moved from Cranston, Rhode Island to Feeding Hills, Massachusetts when I was three years old. As a small family of three, we moved into our brand new home on a very rural and quiet cul-de-sac street. My father had taken a job that required him to relocate to this quaint little town, two hours from all our relatives, especially my beloved Nana. It was a significant transition for my entire family.

It was during this move that I met a special little girl, my age, who lived three houses away from our new home. Brenda mirrored me physically with small features, long full hair and freckled skin. Although I was mesmerized by her twinkling blue eyes, it was her infectious laugh that attracted me to her. As small children, we were girly girls who loved to play dress up, spend endless hours adorning our barbie dolls and acting out make-believe games. Through those years we shared so many wonderful life adventures that brought about a tying bond of sisterhood between us. As we grew older, we shared kindergarten, brownie girl scouts, and elementary school events as if we were one soul.

As age would allow us more liberties, we would meet in the woods behind our houses, at the "Climbing Tree" and tell each other our deepest secrets. The climbing tree, which was an old stubby pine tree, was magical to us because it metaphorically was our spot to share all the things we could never tell another person.

As we sat next to each other on our bus rides home from school, Brenda would whisper to me cupping her hand over my ear.

"Meet me at the climbing tree."

I would respond with a silent nod filled with excitement.

Once off the bus, we would race to our homes and change into our play clothes and then run to our secret place. There we would climb the thick barked branches and find our sitting spots and laugh and chat for hours. The only telltale signs of where we had been was the occasional pine pitch that stuck to our hands and knees as we scaled its gnarly trunk.

Even as we grew and spread our wings and pursued two totally different paths, our neighborhood held a special place within our hearts. Age had no ownership of us there as kindred feelings tethered us to our home base.

The threads of kindred spirits are those treasured threads that knot their first weave in a kismet fashion. It is akin to the Threads of Friendships, yet has a deeper heft to it. It is this form of connection in our tapestry that has a significant attachment to our spiritual self. Kindred spirits are two people that create a special bond between them which is based upon similar experiences and feelings. They are intertwined by energy and attraction.

The Threads of kindred spirits are the cornerstone of our purpose in life providing us with light, love and compassion. When we experience this thread, especially in our childhood years, it brings us to a place of deep nostalgia, safety and a longing to return home. These resilient threads should be treasured and kept in a sacred space for they are a positive connection to our inner self.

THE THREADS OF SAYING GOODBYE

"Goodbyes are only for those who love with their eyes. Because for those who love with heart and soul there is no such thing as separation."

~ *Rumi*

Many years ago, my family adopted a 5-month-old golden retriever puppy. He was the runt of his litter, and we were told had been returned three times because his previous owners said he was "not right." Physically, he was a beautiful puppy with soft amber colored fur and deep brown eyes. He came by the name of Charlie, but my family felt it did not fit him, so we renamed him Casey.

From the minute I laid eyes on him alone in a dog pen, it was kismet. He would come to the side of the dog pen and instead of greeting your hand head first, he would sit, his back facing you and turn his head. He drank from his water bottle the same way, backward. I immediately understood him and embraced all of his nuances with an appreciation of the level of special that he was. Casey and I were inseparable and it became very evident that he hated to be apart from me.

Truth be told, he was an awkward dog. My neighbor, an English woman with a comical but pragmatic demeanor, would say in her thick English accent, "Judy, Casey is not normal."

And I couldn't disagree. He had an old soul persona and was distinctly un-doglike. He did not bark or play catch. He loved his stuffed toys, but never chewed them. Rather, he would gently carry them in his mouth and place them carefully where he lay. He never engaged other dogs, walked off leash from day one, and I became the center of his universe. He loved our family, every member, but only I could walk him on a leash. He ate quietly and rarely begged, except for holidays when Grandpa would sneak him goodies under the table. Casey was completely and utterly the perfect dog, aside from the fact he had terrible skin allergies. He required great care and I tended to his suffering with special diets, medicines, and holistic bath treatments.

Through the years we went, side by side. We walked every Sunday morning, regardless of the weather, in a local state forest park with Rebecca, a dear friend of mine, and her black lab mix, Tasha. Tasha, a vibrant and energetic dog, connected with Casey and they became great friends. They would forage through the trails, Tasha in the lead, running leaps and bounds ahead. Casey would always get about twenty feet away and suddenly look back to see where I was. If I was not near, he would wait or come running back to me. I would send him back onto the path ahead, encouraging him to go have fun and blaze a trail. But Casey would not go any farther than twenty feet.

As the years went by, it got to a point that Casey would hold onto the edge of my sleeve whenever we walked. He would hold the fabric gently between his teeth as if to say, "I will always know where you are if I keep your sleeve in my mouth." I would return home with my right sleeve saturated with saliva, but never once torn.

On one of our regular jaunts with Rebecca and Tasha, I noticed Casey was particularly hesitant to leave my side.

"I don't know what I will do the day Casey has to leave me forever," I said. "He is petrified to leave my side. What happens if he won't cross over? I don't want him alone looking for me."

Rebecca contemplated this and clearly took it to heart. She told her husband my quandary and on our next walk she shared his solution. "When the time comes, give him a sleeve to go with."

His suggestion seemed so right. Someday, God forbid, when the day came I would give Casey a sleeve to hold on to.

Time marches forward and eventually that cold November day arrived. We had walked our last walk in the woods. During that hike, he struggled to walk far, but did his best. He constantly looked back at me, as if to say, "We don't have many more walks together, Mom."

When he looked back at me a final time, clearly struggling with his walk, I snapped a picture of him. It was a poignant picture, his features were so clear, old white-muzzled face, thick amber fur, and dark, tired eyes. The fall leaves in their oranges, yellows, and reds, and the river, running as smooth as glass beside us, provided the perfect backdrop. My shadow is also present in the picture. Even in that frame of captured, frozen reality we were still together. He looked again at me and smiled his cute smile as if to say, "Remember me as I do you."

Two weeks later I was saying goodbye to my beloved golden boy. As he lay on the table, so sick with what was diagnosed as liver failure, I looked at his face, so sweet and kind. We had been through so much together and he meant the world to me. I reached into my pack and pulled out my golden retriever tee shirt and gently placed the sleeve in his mouth. The vet told me it was time to say goodbye. I gathered up every ounce of fortitude I had, kissed his forehead, and whispered in his ear, "take my sleeve along the way, my sweet boy."

He died right then in my arms.

As sad as saying goodbye may have been, I was able to find some comfort in our final goodbye. I no longer feared his being lost on the other side. I knew, in that instant, that he would not be far from me and would most definitely be waiting for me when it was my time to pass. I think of him often and I still miss him. I know I will never know that level of love and devotion again. But I am blessed with the thread that allowed us to walk together in his final moments with his favorite sleeve to hang onto.

The thread of saying goodbye always seems to be thought of with a dark and a heavy weave. It is a thread that not many like to envision within their tapestries. The thought of saying goodbye, no matter the circumstances, is often met with sadness and anxiety, whether it be departing on a business trip, ending a relationship, or saying our final goodbyes, it is always met with the same basic question: Will I see you again?

For me, this thread was one of the harder ones to visualize as soft and pliable. In my mind, I see it as light in color, and of varying hefts. In discovering this emotional thread, I have been able to see my picture more clearly and have developed a greater perception of what life is about. It is about making the most of the moment of saying goodbye, meeting it with a more hopeful mind, and designing that moment with a more colorful and softer texture.

Nothing is certain in life and no one knows all of the answers. The longing and desire to see someone again, even if we are only separated for a short time, is a pain we must all accept. The thread of saying goodbye cushions that acceptance with a sense of hope, love, and the belief that we will see each other again.

THE THREADS OF DISAPPOINTMENT

"When it comes to life, we spin our yarn, and where we end up is really, in fact, where we always intended to be."

~ *Julia Glass*

After our Casey passed away, I literally could not think of getting another dog. But about a year and a half later, I started peeking at the opportunity to adopt from a shelter or rescue. My neighbor, Karen, was an advocate for rescue dogs and when she got the green light to show us some opportunities, a floodgate opened, and a plethora of dog pictures and stories came across my desk. If there is an animal in need of saving, Karen was right in the thick of it!

As I poured over all of the pictures, I started to narrow down my search. My criteria were: male, at least a year old, and golden retriever or golden mix.

Years back when we chose Casey, he shared a pen with a rescue mate, a Great Pyrenees named Callie. My family had gone back and forth between wanting both dogs, but picked Casey because he was best suited for our lifestyle at the time. But we always talked about Callie and how much we wanted her as well.

Karen came over one afternoon with a picture of a rescue dog named Coconut. He was a 15-month-old male, half golden retriever and half Great Pyrenees. He was perfect. I instantly fell in love with him and filled my application out immediately. Karen sent it in the next day and spoke personally to the rescue, using her name and recent adoption as a reference. We were contacted within several days and told we were one of two homes being considered for Coconut. I was so sure that between my phone interview and Karen's recommendations that I was a shoe-in to adopt the pup.

But the following day, I received the news that our family had not been selected to adopt him. I was crushed. Truthfully, I could not believe it. Karen was extremely disappointed as well. We sat down at the drawing board again and looked at countless pups, but my heart just wasn't in it.

Karen continued the hunt, but backed off some because I was no longer as receptive to the whole process as when we had started. I visited local shelters and still, nothing came of it.

Luckily for me, Karen, is a tenacious little woman with the biggest heart of anyone I know. She walked across the street one morning with a picture of two puppies from a litter of seven. Although we had wanted an older male dog, the puppies were very similar in appearance to Casey, only white. One was a male, the other a female. Something pinged my heart when I looked at them, and the rest of my family was equally smitten. We sent an application out to this new rescue in hopes of getting one of the two.

In the days that followed, I grew a little impatient. I wasn't sure my heart could take the hurt of losing out again, so I sent an email to the rescue head inquiring about the status of my application. Over the next few days, I received multiple responses, all saying practically the same thing, all from the same woman at the rescue.

Then the woman called me.

"Ms. Cosby, I want to thank you for all of your emails, but I promise, if anything changes with your application, I will let you know."

"All of my emails?" I replied. "I only emailed you once, but you keep replying to it!"

Turns out, she answered my original email, and thought she had deleted it from her inbox. She could not explain it and we laughed about it, but I knew it was kismet!

Over the next few weeks, we went through the phone interview and home visit. Shortly after that, our application was approved and we adopted our little Maggie Mae.

We were completely in love with our newest family member. I created a Facebook page called the "Magnificent Seven" specifically for the families who adopted the other six pups along with the fosters and rescue agency. It has been a wonderful outlet to check in on the progress of all siblings and to air any questions we had regarding their health. They are an amazing group of people, all of whom live in the New England area. Because of our close proximity, we have been able to have birthday reunions for the pups.

That adoption process, the group of people I now know because of this adoption, and the Facebook page have become a bigger part of our lives than I could have ever imagined!

I know if I had adopted Coconut I would still be writing how much I love him, but my journey was meant to be even better. I was meant to meet and become involved with the group of owners, adopt two dogs, and become involved with rescues. And now I know that Coconut was placed where he was meant to be.

Sometimes the things we truly want don't surface the way we anticipate, but if we would only just allow our destined path to emerge and follow it, what is usually waiting on the other side is something beyond our wildest dreams. Often, we will find that our disappointment leads us to bigger and better things.

We have all been disappointed in our lives at one time or another. It could be something small like finding out your favorite dish is no longer on the menu, or something as big as not getting the job or promotion you worked hard for. But no matter the scale or cause, accepting the letdown and seeing it as a chance for something different or better is what this thread allows us to do.

There is no magic wand, however. The key to dealing with disappointment is simply to get through that moment so that we can regain our perspective and look for those improved possibilities on the other side. Imagine the thread as knotted and dark and the weave misshapen and stunted in the growth and expansion of our tapestry. As tough as it may be, disappointment is a part of life. It shows us that life design requires dimensions of darkness and knotting to help us grow. As we accept the disappointment and acknowledge its sting, we move on and allow the path to proceed to the next place, letting the knots untie and smooth into another area.

I am a true believer that even if the disappointment feels unbearable, there is always a reason for the path we are placed upon. I believe in a greater purpose and lesson in everything. If we turn our minds to that idea, we allow our tapestries to grow not just in width but in depth also. The colors become more enhanced in their richness and the lessons learned through the disappointment can be extremely invaluable in future weaves.

THE THREADS OF FOLLOWING YOUR OWN HEART

"It's impossible," said pride. "It's risky," said experience. "It's pointless," said reason. "Give it a try," whispered the heart."

~ *Author unknown*

An impulsive moment led me to put in an application for a 15-month-old Great Pyrenees named Tobin. I can't tell you why I needed to do it.

After we adopted Maggie Mae, my life was full of family and animals. Every part of my life was full of crazy turmoil and mayhem. My oldest daughter had moved back home with her two cats, my youngest daughter was living at home and commuting to college, and my husband and I were both working full-time jobs. The house chores were crushing me and it was almost impossible to find any quiet time. On those rare occasions when I found a moment to myself, for fun, I would peruse the rescue site where we had found Maggie Mae. I would study the pictures and stories of all of the pups looking for a home and my heart would just be overwhelmed. My husband had already thrown the gauntlet and decreed there would be no more adopting of anything. Yet here I was, clicking through the pages as if there was something calling to me.

As I combed through the pictures, one sweet doggie face called out to me like no other. It was a simple headshot of a Great Pyrenees down in Texas named Tobin. His face was soft and kind. His mouth curled into a smile as the sun hit his bulbous white forehead. But it was his eyes that got me. They were smiling outside, but so sad inside.

I went on to look at other pictures, but always seemed to come back to Tobin and his sad eyes. I showed his picture to my family and everyone thought he was cute. I let it go, assuming someone would surely adopt him.

Days went by and I did not see him on the initial blogs. Then by some fortuitous happening, he kept showing up on my web page. It was as if Tobin was calling me out in his picture. His description was basic and did not give a full history of his rescue or mention if he was good with other animals. All that was indicated was that he was found loose and brought to a high kill shelter. This kill shelter had a policy that if the dog is not claimed within 72 hours they would be euthanized. At zero hour, the rescue was alerted and they answered the call and Tobin was given a second chance at life. I just knew instinctively that he was mine.

I quickly downloaded the rescue application from their site and began the tedious task of filling out the three-page form. Once I started the application, I realized what I really wanted was a chance to foster a dog so that I could get a proper sense of whether multiple dogs were an option for my family. And I wanted my first rescue foster to be Tobin.

I finished the application and went to press send, but hesitated. What was I doing? *This is crazy,* I thought to myself. I minimized the application on my screen and went right to bed, relieved that I had come to my senses. There was no way my family could possibly handle another dog.

The next morning as we ate breakfast together I told my husband what I had almost done.

"I'm glad you came to your senses," he said, placing his coffee on the table, and giving me a raised-eyebrow stare.

That is when I felt a tug of my thread. It literally pulled a knot on the edge of my tapestry and began its own weave. I had no control of its direction, only that I needed to act. It was as if the laptop on the kitchen table held a tug of war strand that would pull me to it and then I would pull myself back.

I finished getting ready for work and grabbed my lunch out of my fridge. I slipped on my heels, placed my sunglasses atop my head, and headed through the kitchen toward the front door. I caught sight of my laptop in my peripheral vision as I passed. I stopped and stepped backward. The application was still there, minimized on my tool bar. Compulsively, I opened it back up and read it over, my mouse hovering over the submit button. Then, as if something possessed my hand, I clicked the button and off went my application into the universe.

By the time I got to work, clocked in, and sat at my desk, the agency had contacted me that they were thrilled I had applied, and by noon I had been approved. After speaking with the rescue agency, I explained that I did not think I was in a position to adopt the dog because of the three cats currently residing with us, but that I would love to foster.

"I think we can make that happen," the woman from the rescue said.

My heart jumped for joy. I had my chance to see this adventure through with the option of returning him for adoption if he was not good with cats or if it was not meant to be.

Two days later, we drove the two hours north to Vermont to pick up the white prince with the sad, soulful eyes. The whole time, I sat hardly believing what I was doing, but knew I had been drawn to this soul for a reason. We met him and his current foster for the first time near a beautiful lake flanked by a scenic mountain. He had just arrived from Texas the day before. He looked up at us as we descended the incline to meet them and he immediately ran over to me and placed his head between my thighs. He greeted my husband and daughter as if we had been together forever. It became apparent that we had a deep connection to each other and even our Maggie took to him instantly.

During the first two weeks he lived in our home, I worked with Tobin to improve his weakened state with short walks and good food. I groomed him and socialized him with Maggie. He had not had experience with cats, and we now had three. It was a struggle to keep him from chasing them, but he handled the meetings very well. He went on car rides and visited people and started to really blossom in those few days. Everyone who met him remarked about how special he was and that he had an old soul persona.

Our lives, although embroiled in the mayhem of logistics, finances, and medical issues, could not resist the pull of the thread that had been cast and the adventure of fostering Tobin. He had been called to our family and the weave of his presence was sewn amongst our individual tapestries.

As everyone who met him in those first two weeks predicted, we adopted Tobin. He wanted us. I know this. His spirit called with a mighty cast of a large white thread that I could not resist catching. We wove that thread into our lives. I promised Tobin that his memories of the kill shelter in Texas would be just that, distant and eventually forgotten, for he would live every day with us, loved and cherished. I whisper in his ear every morning, "you are so loved."

Those who know me would have no trouble believing that I am a very cautious, stay-in-the-box kind of person. I like routine and knowing what to expect in life. Adventure is exhilarating, but is always met with reservation. Before the adventure of fostering and adopting Tobin, my tapestry picture was missing out on greater depth and meaning because of my fear of following my heart.

While we struggled a bit through the transition of adjusting to our newest addition, for all of us, Tobin filled the gap. Even my husband can't imagine life without his "little" buddy. Maggie Mae is completely a different dog with Tobin by her side. Their attraction and love for each other was instantaneous. I followed my heart and it brought me, and those I care about, a greater love than I could ever have imagined.

When your heart and mind call you to do something that is out of the norm, something that may even put your life in turmoil, there is often nothing you can do but to heed the call and have faith that you are following a predestined, fateful path. This thread has no distinct color or texture until you are in the meld of the weave.

Following your heart does not necessarily mean you are being emotional or impetuous. It simply means you have an inner voice that is urging you to turn in a direction you might not have otherwise considered. It is on the same level as destiny and impacts your life with such beautiful experiences. Keeping your heart open to such chance meetings and situations can only make your picture grow in boundless ways.

THE THREADS OF BEING OPEN

"Open your eyes to the beauty around you, open your mind to the wonders of life, open your heart to those who love you, and always be true to yourself."

~ *Donna Davis*

I received an email from the dog rescue that had brought Maggie Mae and Tobin into our lives, asking if I would help in the process of retrieving a previously adopted puppy. The rescue had adopted out a three-month pointer mix to a woman who, unfortunately, was not who she said she was. Her references had provided nothing but positive feedback and she had made a favorable impression on the rescue team. But shortly after the transport of the puppy, the rescue realized they had been misled. The adoption fee check bounced, and they were unable to contact her. Her phone had been disconnected and her address was no longer valid. The veterinarian listed on her application had not seen the puppy or been in contact with the individual after the adoption. For five agonizing months, the rescue searched for the puppy, fearing the worst. Then news arrived that the woman agreed to release the pup to the rescue to avoid further prosecution. The woman's son had agreed to return the puppy to the rescue on the designated date.

As I read through the email that detailed the case history, I was instantaneously committed to the prospect of rescuing the pup from the unfortunate circumstance of her adoption. It required me to drive to another state and temporarily care for her before helping to convey her to the rescue located in Vermont. It was quite the endeavor, but my heart was committed and I gave little thought to what it meant to me to take this on.

In the beginning, I was extremely open to the prospect of retrieving and fostering this pup, but as the days progressed, I became increasingly wary of the position I had put myself in. I was going to go to a home I had little knowledge of with the possibility of picking up an 8-month-old puppy that could be in poor condition. I felt my openness fleeting away, replaced with self-doubt.

Instead of letting the fear rule me, I took charge. I contacted the rescue and began asking questions regarding the person I would be meeting and the circumstances of our transaction. The plan was to meet at a pet store in a town halfway between my location and where the puppy was currently living.

As the date moved closer, I replaced my uncertainty with openness and a willingness to help, never veering from the true meaning of why I accepted this task in the first place. I drove to the pet store with my husband and daughter, and at the specified time, a young man and woman walked in with a very emaciated and scared looking pup. My heart lurched. I walked over confidently and said thank you for surrendering the dog and doing the right thing. He handed me her leash and relinquished the dog. He clearly felt relieved and I could tell that he was very kind and concerned for the puppy's well-being.

My heart immediately filled with a love for this little soul. Angel was slightly built, with thin features. She was white and liver-colored, with beautiful, amber eyes. Her long, thin tail whipping everything in sight with excitement.

The pup stared up at me with trusting eyes, nervously wagging her tail, but clearly very scared. She was completely open to me and we had an instantaneous bond. What brewed behind those thoughtful eyes, I could not tell. It was if she knew that the unknown adventure that was about to occur was her chance for a new and happy life.

We began our drive home shocked at her thin and clearly neglected appearance. Before we even made it to the highway, she vomited on the seat and we realized she was extremely nervous.

In her weakened and nervous state, we knew our two large dogs would be too much for her, so we placed her in our dog pen. It was a lovely August day and the weather was warm but not humid. The pen sat under a Redbud tree along a wooded buffer zone in our back yard. As I watched her, it was as if she was hearing and seeing things she had never expected in her little life. We placed a bowl of ice water and a bowl of kibble in the pen along with two large blankets.

One of our dogs had left a ball inside the pen and when she saw it, her lanky body lurched forward, and with expert precision used her paws to navigate the ball around the pen like a professional soccer player. I tossed it in the air and she caught it without missing a beat. Repeatedly lobbing the soft squeaking ball towards her and watching her make her body turn this way and that way to catch it, my daughter and I laughed and laughed. She must have realized she was the object of our joy and I could see that she had begun to feel comfortable with us and our connections to each another.

When the time came for us to take her to the rescue in Vermont, my daughter hugged and kissed her goodbye. I laid a fleece blanket on the back seat of the car and grabbed ice water in a jug and the ball she had played with all afternoon. I placed her on the seat and got in next to her. She looked puzzled for just a second, but soon settled down onto the furry blanket. Within a minute, she had skirted her lithe tiny body next to mine, her delicate paw with untrimmed nails placed gently on my thigh. She closed her eyes as if I was her accepted fate. As she slept, I gently petted her head.

"Dogs are so special," I said to my husband. "At any given time, they give completely of themselves, they trust in us and place their entire fate in our hands, never knowing if we will love them or hurt them."

Angel was proof of that. She had given her open thread a chance to take her somewhere else. I had given my open thread a chance to do a good deed and step out of my safe zone.

When we met up with the woman who would take Angel the rest of the way to the foster waiting for her, Angel was very scared to get out of our car. I watched her curl up in the back seat of the black Toyota after we passed her off, the woman sitting beside her as well. I placed the ball next to her and she took it, looking up at me with unsure eyes.

"You'll be fine sweet girl," I told her. "Soon you'll find a forever home and people who will love you completely."

She put her head down on the blanket and the door closed between us.

I got back in my car, my heart a little achy. I watched the car slowly pull out of the parking lot and on to the main road, heading north. I was instantly struck with a feeling of good and bad all at once.

I had taken a chance and stepped out of my comfort zone and done something truly wonderful with this thread. I'd been able to help this little pup leave a terrible plight and find her deserved happiness. Part of me wished I could have done more, that I could have spent more time with her, but that was not our destiny. We had been allowed to enhance each other's lives for just a day, just long enough for our open threads to meld together and fuse. I felt so alive and good inside and loved the fact that I made a difference in both our lives.

There are so many times that chance situations present themselves and we miss the opportunity to follow the direction of an open thread because we are so busy trying to rationalize the event and proceed on our supposed paths. If we could only realize that each encounter is a wonderful way to add color and texture to the beauty of the tapestry we create. The linking of those tapestries with these weaves can result in such an exquisite picture.

There are so many opportunities that can lead to these life-changing adventures. Always be open to the chance meetings that can enhance your life and bring deeper meaning to the richness of your tapestry. The slightest of meetings can be sent to us for so many reasons. Do not be afraid or closed-minded to the depth of these gifts. Practice being open so that you can see the world with new and fresh eyes

THE THREADS OF OUR GIFTS

"Stir the world with your skills, shake the world with your talents, move the world with your brilliance, change the world with your genius."

~ *Matshona Dhliwayo*

My cat, Valentine, was a feral kitten that my husband found on the side of the road on Valentine's Day. We had dinner plans that night and he was late. I was very concerned until he pulled up with a wet and disheveled kitten wrapped in his new black Nike coat and explained how he'd found her in a puddle in the middle of the road, freezing, injured, and starving.

We called our veterinarian, but they were closed. We felt there was no other choice but to take her to an animal shelter, sadly knowing that they would euthanize her if she was too far from saving.

"Please let us know how the kitten makes out," my husband said to the technician as he said his goodbyes.

Three veterinarians worked on Valentine. Two voting for immediate euthanasia. The third, a young veterinarian new to the shelter, decided to take a chance on the little kitten. The next night we got a phone call. The 8-week-old female kitten would require a lot of care to get her better, but she was expected to make a full recovery and would be ready for us to adopt her.

Valentine was the kindest cat I have ever known. She was our miracle cat, our precious blue tabby kitten with the golden mark of fur on her head. We would tell her she was kissed by God. We had 12 fabulous years with her and shared so much love. When she passed in my arms, I was sad to let her go, but I knew we would be together again.

Jameson Bond is a stray black and white tuxedo cat who donned his body and fur like an aristocrat. He made the rounds in our neighborhood, trying to find a warm house, but like a suave "love 'em and leave 'em" type, he never stayed very long after he was fed and bedded down for a night. The four houses he frequented all had a swooning lady of the house, and it became apparent that he had the personality of the famous spy 007 James Bond. He was friendly and wild all at the same time.

The way he entered our lives was completely in keeping with his personality.

I had spied him drinking water from our koi pond on an Indian Summer day in early October. I say drinking, but knowing him, he was probably trying to catch and eat my koi! Our dog Casey, an unusually gentle soul who had no interest in any animals, simply walked by the cat, did his business and jumped on the deck to come back in through our atrium door. Like a thief looking for an unlocked door, Jameson saw his chance and rushed by Casey and into our living room! He rubbed against my leg and purred so intensely. At first, I fretted over the fact that he could be rabid or flea-bitten, but he soon romanced his way into my good graces.

His entrance into our lives at that time turned out to be an unforeseen gift. Eight weeks later, we lost our Casey. Jameson helped to ease our pain during those lonely days. His gift to our tapestry came during the fall season. His threads creating colors of oranges, reds, yellows, black, and white—all strong hues to bolster a family.

The incredible thing about Jameson was that the morning he arrived at our door, not an hour before, I had awoken from bed after an intense dream. In the dream, my nana had come to me carrying a cat.

"You make a lot of noise in heaven, but you rarely see the signs sent," she said and handed me the cat.

"Nana, you have given me back my Valentine!" As I looked at the cat I realized it was not Valentine at all and put the cat down on the ground.

The cat began to rub up and down my left leg, back and forth, arching its back higher and higher, trying to reach me.

"This is not Valentine, Nana!" I said, almost ungratefully. "You gave me the wrong cat!"

To which my grandmother replied while pointing her bony index finger at me, "Heed your signs!"

I awoke from the dream and told my husband about the cat. Not an hour later, Jameson Bond was sweet-purring his way into our lives. When I looked down at him, I noticed a heart-shaped spot on his nose. This cat was not my beloved Valentine, but he donned the mark that meant her name.

There have been so many animals who have had an impact on my life, too many to mention them all. But in the experience that has come from my interaction with each of them, I accepted and embraced the fact that I have a gift for loving animals. In that love, comes a host of animals, many of whom have found me in the most interesting of ways. They are gold, black, white, grey, orange, and brown and they are linked to my being.

Our lives are marked by an array of natural gifts and shortcomings. Both are integral parts of who we are. It is vitally important to embrace these qualities and somehow color them in your mind. In recognizing and responding to our talents, we must take note of what our strengths are and how to truly maximize them.

Our gifts don't have to be significant or newsworthy, but they should be recognized and utilized. Some of our gifts are more spiritual, technical, or creative. The importance is to recognize the talents God has given us and use them to make a difference in our own life and to significantly affect the lives of those around us. These gems of our personality are the strands that will color our tapestry with richness and allow the edges to be woven into a greater capacity. Don't be afraid to harness your legacies and make them greater. Caring for people or animals, or being able to perform creative or athletic works, are all examples of the gifts bestowed upon us, and what we do with them is our contribution to the infinite masterpiece.

THE THREADS OF DESPAIR

*"Run your fingers through my soul. For once, just once, feel
exactly what I feel, believe what I believe, perceive as I perceive,
look, experience, examine, and for once; just once, understand."*

~ *Author Unknown*

The threads of despair are strands that I have only witnessed from
the outside looking in. It is the stitch that I fear most. It comes from
immeasurable loss. I have an empathic nature when I see true loss in
the eyes of those that carry it. I often feel their emotions with my entire
body. To the naked eye, these people dress, act, and participate in life as
if nothing is wrong. They can laugh, cry, or even work alongside you, but
when you look in their eyes, there is a blankness, an emptiness. Their
pain is so deeply penetrating it is as if you are looking into a pool of
water but you can only see the reflection that masks the deep waters
within.

A friend of mine lost her child in an accident. It immobilized her.
She is still a beautiful woman, still an incredible mom to her other
children, an amazing wife, and a hard-working employee at her job. But
there was no hiding the pain in her eyes. Every time I see her I can see
the reflection of the strands of her despair. They conflict with every
breath she takes.

I have seen my own despair, but only after a friend pointed out that
it was there. In the year that followed my father's death, my daughter

Catherine began her fight with her illness, and our beloved golden retriever passed away. I spent a year enduring what seemed to be perpetual heartache.

At some point during that year, we decided to take a family photo for our Christmas card. Our background, clothes, and smiles were just beautiful. The four of us sat together on our floor in front of our atrium door with the beautiful scenery behind us. We looked so happy.

I could not wait to share the beautiful image, and forwarded a copy to my friend.

She emailed me back a short time later. "Such a beautiful picture of you all, but your eyes looked sad despite your pretty smile."

I pulled up the picture and looked at it again. My smile was genuine, being together was a gift, but she was right, my eyes gave me away. They did not smile or show any emotion. They reflected the moment, but inside I was a mess. She was able to see a glimpse of my deep loss and despair and now, I could too.

Luckily for me, I was able to improve my mindset and get back to who I was prior to the loss. But for some, their eyes will depict this heartbreaking stitch for long periods of time, if not forever and those who witness it will never forget it.

None of us are immune from the burden of this thread. We may catch a glimpse of it, but it is not apparent to all. At times, a very light wisp like the threads of a cobweb may touch us, and we may become aware of its presence. But for most, it is buried and hidden from view.

There are, however, some lives that begin their day in a sad place. Their pain and heartache are so strong and so entirely embroiled in their day-to-day lives, that even breathing takes effort. Significant loss, particularly the loss of a child, can create a tapestry that doesn't allow the same level of light to shine or radiate from within ever again. Threads produced from such an experience do not reflect light or emit color. The strand, lackluster and dark, runs its weave through the base of the cloth, anchoring the loss in every stitch. Its presence is permanent and unchangeable, but kindness, compassion, love, and care may soften it.

THE THREADS OF EMOTIONAL GROWTH

"Let us always meet each other with a smile, for the smile is the beginning of love."

~ Mother Teresa

On a quick trip to the grocery store on the way home from work, I haphazardly gathered the items I needed, tossing them into my basket as I scurried through the aisles and hurried to the express lane. I was short on time and impatient, to say the least. In line in front of me was a very elderly man. He was alone and had about ten items on the conveyer belt. With slow methodical movements, he opened his wallet. He appeared flustered and anxious. His gnarled and thickly veined hands fumbled to open his billfold and carefully remove the dollar bills he had neatly tucked inside. His thin white hair was mostly hidden beneath a black and white checkered wool cap and because his stature was slight, his khaki colored cargo overcoat enveloped his entire body. I huffed for a moment and quickly scanned the other lines to see if I could just switch to another register.

"I'm sorry, sir, you don't have enough to cover the charge. You're short $2.00," said the cashier.

In that instant, his demeanor changed to one of embarrassment. With unsteady, trembling hands, he released what money he had to the cashier and started to reach for a roll of paper towels to put back.

I envisioned my own father standing in this line. How would I want him to be treated? It was then that I realized that these moments are what life is all about. Time is key and it rules us in a way that is beyond our control. I quickly whipped out a $5 bill and handed it to the clerk and told her to put the paper towels back into his order. He looked up at me almost puzzled.

"You would do that for me?" he asked.

"Of course," I said softly.

He replied in almost a whisper, "You really would do that for me? Thank you." His warm grin beamed with his gratitude and his sad, blue, aging eyes twinkled.

As the clerk took the change out of the register and proceeded to hand it into my direction I shook my head. "No, the change is his."

He looked almost stunned and tried to decline, but I insisted and the clerk was more than happy to oblige.

I watched him slowly walk away towards the exit with his bag of groceries in hand.

I took care of my groceries and made it to my next destination in plenty of time. I know there is a reason for the concept of paying it forward, but there is also a benefit. Those few moments colored my tapestry in such a way that I wanted to continue to feel that feeling. I wanted my soul to be colored with goodness and kindness and even though there would be days to challenge me, and some that would even see me fail, my odds of creating a beautiful picture of my spiritual-self were greater. Even now, when I think of that day, it makes me smile. I still recall his steely blue eyes.

When the pictorial vision of your tapestry has been formed in your mind, it is always helpful to conceptualize what you look like within the composition. Dig deep and find the vision of your mind, body, and soul. It is the pulsing color that comes from within you. Try to envision that place, whether it is in your heart, your abdomen, or your head and the color that is sent forth from you. Imagine your fingers as the way your threads touch and weave into another's tapestry. The threads literally flowing from your fingertips to everything you touch. Conceptualize how the words you speak look as threads as they flow from your mouth and blend with another's tapestry.

When you start to see yourself in this way, you realize how much your actions and words mingle with others. You can witness how just a brief encounter can create a picture of kindness or a picture of hurt. If we were more readily able to see our actions and words in the form of colorful imagery, we would most likely take the time to carefully construct ourselves in a kinder and gentler fashion.

THE THREADS OF OVERCOMING

"It is by fighting the limitations, temptations, and failures of the world that we reach our highest possibilities."

~ Helen Keller

There are some that must travel a road enshrouded in the kind of blackness that requires fortitude and faith to traverse through and find the light again. Addiction is a level of darkness that truly never goes away, and depending on the journey chosen, is the road that can be laced with pitfalls forever. A family friend had an alcohol addiction that took his household to the brink of collapse. That is what addiction does. It steals everything away from the addict and destroys all of those around who love them.

His family and friends had no concept of how to remove it and repair the damage. The harder they tried, the worse it got.

Then one day he contacted me.

"I need to come over and talk to you. Is this a good time?" he asked with despair in his voice.

"Of course it is, come over now," I said, not fully understanding the gravity of what was about to be shared.

We sat together at my kitchen table as silence hung between us. I knew something had been wrong, but I did not expect the words that were uttered at that moment.

He sat still, head bowed down staring at his folded hands neatly placed atop the table.

"I think I have a drinking problem. I don't know what to do. I know I have lost control of everything around me and have hurt my family," he said with deep pain in his voice.

I sat for a moment, my mind racing. How do I respond to this? What do I say or do that will help him?

"I need help." He looked up with pleading, tear-filled eyes.

I reached over the table and clasped his hands in mine.

"Admitting you have a problem is the first step in getting better," I said with conviction in my voice. "We will find you a professional to talk with and look up local AA meetings for you to attend. Would you like me to go with you?" I offered.

His lips quivered, an audible sob left his mouth, as he softly uttered a "yes."

That night he began his passage towards sobriety.

Those first few weeks were wrought with anxiety and pain. We found a therapist who would be able to guide him through the path of recovery. As promised, I went with him to his first AA meeting, as well as many that followed. It was a momentous experience, physically for him, and spiritually for both of us.

That first AA meeting was held in the basement of a local town church. As we walked to the doorway he was immediately greeted by warm, smiling faces. With my hand gently placed on his back to give him reassurance, we walked together into the hall and sat.

As the meeting began my heart raced. I knew that this was a unique journey and one filled with self-reflection and acceptance. I sat and listened, in awe of the remarkable people that were gathered in that room. These people, all from different walks of life, sat unified by the hope for recovery and healing. It was very clear that night that addiction does not discriminate.

Then came the moment of truth. As the introductions moved along the room, my friend stood.

He stated his name out loud and said these powerful words "And I am an alcoholic."

I looked up at him from my seated position and smiled. It was the most bittersweet of smiles. It held the realization of the long, difficult path ahead and the admiration I had for his courage.

As his journey began, family and friends educated themselves on the disease of alcoholism and how to be both effective and supportive of his recovery while protecting their own personal space. Through the journey, they learned how to recognize the warning signs of relapse and live within the boundaries of recovery. Through the thread of overcoming, there is a level of learning that teaches us that those with addiction issues are not bad people, that their families are not uncaring, and that there is no shame in it if you are willing to pursue recovery and dedicate yourself to sobriety. He is now thankful to live a sober life and his family is grateful to be positively affected by his recovery as well.

We are all given our burdens. In every life, the rain falls. Developing the resources to productively assist the addicted and sharing that knowledge positively can create a successful coalition. There is no room for enabling or for being unsupportive. Making a constructive impact with whatever is bestowed upon us, good or bad, enhances our lives' pictures and allows our tapestries to weave its fraying edges into another's.

It was when he admitted he needed help that a light sparked and a door opened. It was not the family demanding of him anymore, it was him setting and pursuing his own self-expectations. The arduous work of overcoming addiction had begun and the pathway to sobriety was on the horizon. With each step of recovery was a thread of hope to weave into the bands of anguish and hardship. With each month of sobriety came the resilience of strength. It was, and is, a journey that would have highs and lows and be a forever commitment. Relationships that had been ruined or affected also blended together, healing and rejoining their tapestries. The threads of overcoming had been forged.

Hope is the key to the threads of overcoming and it is alive within the twine of life. When life hits you with an unexpected turn and the thought of dealing with pitfalls beyond your control are before you, the thread of overcoming should be pulled from the spool of life and purposely sewn into the fabric of your masterpiece. All will need to draw from the thread at certain times. Serious illness, death, and financial disaster are examples of hardships that require the thread of overcoming. The fortitude, hope, and support are the factors that make this thread bolster within our tapestry.

When the thread of overcoming is needed and the first stitch sewn into our tapestry the strength it draws is immeasurable, allowing us the chance to triumph over our affliction and change the course of our lives in so many ways.

THE THREADS OF ORIGIN

"I believe in the old, because it shows us where we come from – where our souls have risen from. And I believe in the new, because it gives us the opportunity to create who we are becoming."

~ Abigail Washburn

I have a beloved family friend, Minnie, who is as dear to me as one could be. She has been a part of my life and a friend to my entire family since the day I was born. We are bonded in a way that transcends all levels of what defines family.

A fun-loving soul, she traverses her life with lightness and humor. Minnie is a beautiful woman with deep brown eyes and an incredible smile that could light the sky. She is well read and spoken and has always been a fashion icon with her trendy attire. Minnie traveled extensively, owned beautiful homes and drove the nicest cars including a funky purple Volvo. My love for her is boundless and she has always been a role model for me.

"I am the product of an unwanted pregnancy," she shared with me one day as we sat chatting about life. "My birth parents, who I never knew, put me up for adoption."

Shocked by this revelation I did not know quite what to say. I was an adult when this was shared with me and although it changed nothing between us, I could not help but wonder how this had affected her life.

"Did that make you sad?" I questioned.

"No, not at all," she stated. "I was fortunate enough that they made that decision and I was adopted by a set of very loving parents."

"Didn't you want to know all about them? What they looked like? Where they were from?" I questioned in rapid succession.

She pondered for a moment and then smiled. "I am here for a reason. I was blessed to have my adoptive parents who gave me a very good life. Because of that adoption, I was able to meet your mother and be a part of your life."

Although her birth parents had no contribution to her life's journey, the impact of their interaction had brought her into the world. She had been adopted as an only child by a loving family. She had been told the truth of her birth and how she came to be. Her adoptive parents continually shared how she was a gift to them and they loved her as their own. Although she was aware of the facts of her birth, she had no ideas or visuals of her biological parents. She only knew the love and care of the ones who had raised her. Her speculation about her birth parents had no impact on her grand picture because of the lack of interaction with them.

Through the years, we would wonder if Minnie had inherited a similar laugh, voice inflection, and love of the ocean from her birth parents. With all those unanswered questions, she could never really receive the answers, so her bond with them stagnated. Their strand ended with her creation, it did not color, texture, or enlarge her tapestry. This thread bound her long ago to these two individuals, but for her, it knotted and ended where it began.

The thread of origin in our tapestries' foundation is a very personal thread. When this thread is bound into the cloth, it is profound in an entirely different manner from any other thread. It is foundational in that it brings a dimension that other threads can weave around, but it is quiet and exerts very little influence on our lives. It is an initial thread that is created with no emotional attachment and is present at the formation of our basic life picture. It is simply the thread that produced our creation.

THE THREADS OF GOODNESS

"A single act of kindness throws out roots in all directions, and the roots spring up and make new trees. The greatest work that kindness does to others is that it makes them kind themselves."

~ Amelia Earhart

When I think of goodness, certain individuals come to mind. Their existence is filled with compassionate acts and kindness. They are not perfect, nor do they set out to be of service to others in pursuit of gains of any kind. Instead they lift those around them simply because it is their true nature to do so.

Before retiring, a gentleman who is all of those things, worked in my husband's office. John worked hard, raised his family the best he could, and lived a simple but enjoyable life. Every day was met with a smile and a good intention. He and his wife love to travel and experience new adventures, but they always search for those opportunities to pursue a more fulfilling experience than just simple sightseeing would allow. They have traveled to archeological digs in Italy and worked the sites. They experienced the local culture and saw the countryside on a deep and meaningful level. They also love the extreme conditions of Mount Washington and enjoy skiing together, but always volunteer to be a part of the officiating crew that sets up ski races. The list of these selfless vacations goes on and on.

John is a spiritual man and very involved with his church and its parishioners. He is devoted to helping those in need and does good works within his church family. I met him at one of my husband's many work-related events and could not help but see the true integrity of this man. Every time he walked into a room his smile lit up the space. Tall, slim, and always neatly dressed, he's a bit of a jokester and laughter follows him wherever he goes. I often found myself looking for him at company events because I knew there would be an entertaining evening ahead.

When a neighbor of his had a stroke and was hospitalized, John immediately amassed a group of men, including my husband, to spend their weekend building a ramp for this couple and assist the wife with configuring the first floor of their home to allow the man to comfortably convalesce. John also saw my husband and I through a difficult period in our own lives and was the one who had shared his timeshare in the Berkshires with us when we needed to "get away from it all."

For me, John's continual ability to be a light in the dark and a friend to those around him, serves as an inspiration. The world has more than its fair share of disappointment, pain, and darkness, but so long as the threads of goodness weave their magic into our lives, the world will remain bright. I can only hope to become like John as I continue my life's journey and share my own thread of goodness with those around me.

The threads of goodness are what keep our tapestries images alive and fulfilled. When you envision the threads of goodness, imagine them touching and growing as they create goodwill. They are the threads that our ethics and morals are woven from. It is, however, also the thread that comes with the most challenges and greatest price. These precious threads of goodness can be very easily snipped by the influences of a negative world, and are often targets for those who strive to destroy the light. Remarkably, these threads may be extremely fragile on their own, but when woven into the picture, they can bolster and strengthen any thread they link to.

THE THREADS OF MINDFULNESS

"Begin doing what you want to do now. We are not living in eternity. We have only this moment, sparkling like a star in our hand and melting like a snowflake."

~ Sir Francis Bacon

It was the very last weekend of August 2017. The weather was absolutely perfect, with blue clear skies, low humidity, and temperatures in the mid-70s. My husband, Craig, and I had decided to spend the last remaining days of the ebbing summer in our favorite seaside community. We slept in that Sunday morning taking our time, then readied ourselves for a walk on the beach, dousing ourselves with sunscreen and donning sunglasses and baseball caps. We jogged across the street to the pristine, fluffy sand and the Atlantic Ocean spanning across the horizon. There was no greater joy we could think of than the feel of the sunshine on our skin and hearing the thunderous roll of the crashing waves.

Following a path that lay nestled between patches of tall sea grass, we walked through the main beach entrance. Not far from the entrance was a section of the beach festooned with volleyball nets. The sound of serves and volleys competed with the waves as players practiced and prepared for a tournament that morning. We left the flurry of activity behind us and strolled to a quiet portion of the beach near a little inlet and began our walk along the shoreline.

Groups of seagulls ran in and out of the water, fluffing their feathers and sunning themselves in the warm sand under the rising sun. The sun was at just the right angle to create a mirrored reflection in the veil of sea foam and moist sand beneath it. The deeper, stiller waters looked like glass as far as my eyes could see.

There were other walkers on the beach, talking and embracing the glory of that lazy Sunday morning. Their casual beachwear and sun hats lightly billowing from the fresh sea breeze.

Further up the beach, a grandfather played tag with his three little grandchildren. They laughed and squealed as their grandfather morphed into a child himself and called "you're it."

Dogs ran about chasing invisible prey, young families laughed and frolicked as they played catch-me-if-you-can with the foamy, rolling surf, and the elderly strolled along the water's edge enjoying the quiet pace of the soft beach and uncrowded walkways.

As I walked hand in hand with my husband, I realized how much this little stretch of land brought such a sense of calm and serenity to my life. On that magical day, the sun, sand, and sea transcended their individual reality and combined to bestow a peace upon all those who were present to witness it. Just being in that space and time had given each of us a chance to feel healthy, happy, and at complete ease with life.

Within that shoreline paradise, I became so completely aware of how much that weekend meant to me and how truly grateful I was for the life I had. I took a deep breath trying to absorb every ounce of the peace that surrounded me within the gift of a perfect day.

These threads are not easy to note and are, at times, difficult to incorporate into our day-to-day lives. Not every day will be a walk on the beach, but when you are able to experience this mindful thread it can change how you perceive everything else in your life.

The thread of mindfulness appears when we become acutely aware of the things around us. This awareness does not require a grandness of moment or a particular vibrancy of exchange. Many times, the mindful thread is so small and insignificant that it doesn't even seem to make an impact on our tapestries and is only noticed after the fact. But when we do recognize it, it adds depth and richness to the grand picture.

THE THREADS OF REVISITING PAIN

"The hardest thing to ever do is to reveal the naked soul to the world. However, in doing so brings healing, growth, strength, and powerful inspiration!'"

~ *H. E. Olsen*

I recently witnessed a family member go through an ugly experience of alienation and rejection all because one person decided that she was no longer a welcome member of her family unit. I saw her trying to navigate through her family while being very aware of the rejection. I knew exactly how it felt to walk into a room of family members who distanced themselves from you and showed their disapproval. I had suffered the same experience and it pained me to watch someone else go through that kind of misery.

I could have locked away my experience, kept those old feelings secured in their own space, but by allowing myself to revisit the pain of my past, I was able to reach out to her during those moments and ease her discomfort. Having an ally that supports and stands by you during difficulties like that is the key to getting through them in one piece. I had often wished for someone just like that when I faced my own family struggles.

It wasn't easy to dig up all of those painful memories or reopen a wound I had worked so hard to heal. After all of the heartache I had suffered through, I had proven to myself that I was a far better person, having emerged from that level of hurt. Yet in delving back into that experience, I was forced to look at those threads again, forced to feel their fire, coarseness, and complexity, and was surprised to find them now softer and paler. My perspective and sense of self had changed and those difficult threads no longer had the same effect that they once did.

With the knowledge that there was life after the pain, we shared our feelings together, and she knew I was able to empathize with her. Because I understood her pain and was familiar with her issue, I was able to assist in her healing process and she was able to move forward at a more resilient pace and begin the journey of acceptance.

Although there is a natural aversion to welcoming these threads into our picture, we must be courageous and open to seeing them. We must resist the desire to look away or snip it before it can even knot its first stitch into our fabric. The truth is that without this thread we run the risk of repeating history and allowing ourselves to relive a negative experience again and again in its entirety.

The threads of revisiting pain exist not only to remind us of previous lessons learned, but to allow us to re-examine and bring forth something positive from our past experiences. They are our visual scars and gnarled knots in our tapestries. Looking at them may be unpleasant, but the only way we can keep from becoming a tangled mess is to view the experience of our pain with a higher knowing.

Do not be afraid to look at these strands. In the end, they are the composites that make us whole again.

THE THREADS OF OUR OWN PATHS

"I don't know whether you can look at your past and find, woven like the hidden symbols on a treasure map, the path that will point to your final destination."

~ *Jodi Picoult*

I started my career in human resources with a vivacious young woman who was a dynamo in the recruiting and leadership field. Mary excelled in hiring and career development, where I excelled in the benefits and wellness side. We were fresh out of college and ready to conquer the world. We married at the same time, had our first children weeks apart from each other and then moved our careers to different levels based on our needs at the time.

During those earlier years, I took on part-time positions that halted my career growth so that I could have more flexibility at home. Mary did the opposite, she created her empire and went for it with gusto allowing her family a good solid lifestyle. As life would have it, we lost touch with each other aside from various Christmas cards or chance meetings at restaurants. Then I heard she was taking an early retirement. A mutual friend reached out to me with an invitation for a get-together before Mary moved to Florida. I was shocked to hear that she had decided to halt her career at such a critical time.

During our get-together, I learned that her oldest child was very ill and required full-time care. She had opted to dedicate herself to him and his debilitating illness. My youngest daughter had been just diagnosed with a serious blood disease which would not only rock our family, but require us to travel hours back and forth weekly to Dana Farber in Boston. I had only recently decided to cut back my own work hours.

Our paths had started with passion, energy, and dedication to ourselves and our careers. Twenty-five years later, it had landed us on a similar path again. We talked for hours that night as I learned of her heartache and her choice. I could relate because I was in the same situation.

During this path merge, we have again become a force of support for each other and our friendship has once again tethered our tapestries together. I feel fortunate that God put us on this path together and that Mary and I have connected once more. It is not a road we wished for, but it is one that has allowed us to re-establish and strengthen a binding tie of love and support.

Each one of us has a destiny and a direction unique to our own creation. The paths we take are designed to be followed at our own pace and time. They are a creation of what we are destined to become. Some are surefooted and short, and some are long and uncertain. The key is to learn to accept our calling and enhance it the best we can. Each composite of the path is woven with many varieties of threads and colors.

There are roads that lead us to our goals or roadways we did not even imagine. These paths are doorways to yet another chance to build on what we have been given. Some of these roads are burdens that are completely unwanted. They are dismal, hard, and painful. These roadways are made of the coarsest of threads and tend to be void of bright colors. They are the thoroughfares of grief, regret, pain, addiction, greed, mental illness, malice, and discord. These roads are not meant to be tread on for long.

Other paths are light, colorful, and full of promise. These are the roads that we may walk on often and that we may share with other souls from time to time. These fellow travelers enhance our path with their own threads and colors. These interwoven moments can be extremely detailed and binding. Others may be short and very simple in their color and texture. Some souls weave their threads with us for a short time, separate, and then rejoin our path to finish what was originally woven.

Know that these people are placed on our paths not by accident but because they are meant to be a companion on our journey. Each provides a tool for learning, and sharing the road gives clarity to the endeavor.

THE THREADS OF INTENSE EMOTION

"Those who enter the gates of heaven are not beings who have no passions or who have curbed passions, but those who have cultivated an understanding of them."

~ *William Blake*

At one of the many town meetings my husband and I attended, a proposal was made to install speed humps on our street. The meeting started with a chorus of friendly hellos and smiles from neighbors from the surrounding neighborhood. But as the discussion began over the proposal, things became heated. As each side began to articulate their points, neighbors who were normally very kind and civil began speaking in angry tones.

My husband and I became aware of our own emotional reactions to the discussions and we assisted each other in our ability to be calm and fair as we voiced our opinion. We bolstered each other in those moments and it became very clear to both of us that we had not taken the time to recognize where the emotions were going. We both valued our lovely neighborhood and the people who live within the adjoining streets. Being able to look at the larger picture and seeing my neighbors in a positive light made me recognize that the negativity within me was not healthy.

When we talk ourselves down from the cliff of overreactions, we regain our composure and leave the situation in a more productive light.

When the meeting was over, I was able to walk out with my neighbors and chat with them, regardless of their stance, and remain in good standing with them all. The goal of keeping our intense emotions under control is to be able to walk through a heated situation and end up just as respected on the other side.

Being overly aggressive does not usually bode well for keeping a level head and projecting a positive outcome. Too many times an argument between people quickly escalates for no other reason than a loss of temper. Emotions cloud our judgment and when engaged in an argument, can often leave us with regret.

Threads of intense emotions are woven into our tapestries, and are identifiable, not by the depth of the strand, but by the electric colors they emit. They are the strands of reactions and flash within our tapestries like a neon sign.

These threads define our intense emotion. Passion brings our tapestries to life with a vibrancy of colors and movement. Negative reactions can be very destructive to our picture if not handled appropriately.

When this thread is cast into the fabric of our lives we must learn how to wield it to our advantage or curb its direction to lessen its intensity. Tempering the emotion allows us to weave a more positive outcome.

THE THREADS OF LASTING
IMPORTANCE

"It's not about getting by. It's about the stack of tiny little moments of joy and love that add up to a lifetime that's been worthwhile. You can't measure them; you can only capture them; like snapshots in your mind."

~ *C. Robert Cargill*

My eldest daughter, Sarah, booked a vacation flight to Tucson, Arizona. She would be flying by herself to meet a friend who had already arrived days earlier. As her mother, I was excited for her but at the same time concerned for her safety. We had planned for me to drop her off at the airport for her afternoon flight. My mother asked if she could come with us to see Sarah off on her journey. There we were, three generations of women, chatting and laughing together as we took the scenic route to the airport.

My mother, coming from an age of wisdom and experience was so excited for Sarah. She recalled her days of travel and one trip she took with her friends to Bermuda. She shared how much fun she and her friends had together and a few of their crazy adventures. My mother was appreciative of the youthful experiences this trip would record for my daughter. She was looking into the past and recognizing the gem of this adventure.

Sarah, at her youthful age, was full of anticipation and looked forward to the experience with wide-eyed wonder. She was not weighed down by the worry of what could go wrong; her focus remained firmly rooted in the excitement of what was in store for her. She was only looking forward at a projection of her future.

As the generation between them, I was the proverbial killjoy. I still was able to feel the adventure, but the wary heart of motherhood could also sense all of the things that could go wrong on her trip. I worried about her safety, if she had enough money, if her friends would meet her at the other end with no problems. I was muddied in the present of her situation, but glad she was able to finally realize her dream.

Three separate threads weaving within our own tapestry's yet connecting each one of us to a singular moment and time in my car. We waved our final goodbyes and watched as Sarah made her way through security, a giant smile on her face. She picked up her bag from the x-ray conveyor belt and gave us the thumbs up before disappearing into the terminal.

My mother and I silently walked back to the car and got in. We put on our seatbelts, clicking them closed at almost the exact same time and looked at each other.

"Chinese food?" I asked, suddenly hungry.

She nodded and I called in a take-out order to our favorite restaurant. As we exited the airport parking garage en route to the restaurant, both of us smiled at each other and drove most of the way in silence. Our threads melded together to form this exquisite picture of three women sharing strength, wisdom, and love. We sat on a red cushioned bench at the entrance of the restaurant and my mother decided to order two glasses of white wine. I gladly accepted her spontaneous suggestion.

We lifted our glasses in a toast to Sarah and her journey, and sipped our drinks until the food was ready.

Years later, it would be that memory of her trip, the independence she exhibited, and the simple toast that would resound within the dimensions of our relationship. A lasting, important thread that resonates with our love of Sarah and our love of each other.

Sometimes we are unaware of the importance of threads being woven into our tapestries. They are sewn within the picture as they happen within a multi-faceted moment. In the beginning it is translucent, but as it ages, the color becomes deeper, shimmering just as the event becomes richer and more meaningful with the passage of time.

Always be aware that when weaving your picture, there are many dimensions that are occurring at the same time. Be open to that fact that as you are currently creating your own weave that there are multitudes of threads combining within it.

Live your life with the understanding that while any given moment in time may seem benign and simple, later it may shine with a brilliance you never knew was there. Open your heart to these moments and the potential of their impact on your life. It is not the monumental moments that will strongly impact this thread of lasting importance, it is those stitches made when we are least aware that will shine the most.

THE THREADS OF HUMOR

"Like a welcome summer rain, humor may suddenly cleanse and cool the earth, the air, and you."

~ *Langston Hughes*

When I worked as an administrative assistant in a doctor's office, I would dress meticulously for work every single day. Earrings, necklaces, shoes, and outfits all had to coordinate. One day, I chose a sleeveless navy-blue dress with a black lace cardigan, accessorizing with a large gold link necklace, matching earrings, and black pumps. I did my hair and makeup just so and went off to work. About an hour into my morning I felt something strange under my arm on the left side. I look down and to my surprise, there was a black lace sock stuck to the sweater. I pulled it off and laughed. My co-worker shared in my amusement. Neither of us had noticed the black sock strategically placed so it looked as if it was sewn on my sweater. I wondered how many patients had spotted that sock as they checked in.

About an hour later, I discovered the matching sock, stuck to my sweater under my other arm! My co-worker and I laughed about my stowaway socks for the rest of the day. How easy it would have been to get embarrassed and belittle myself or make myself feel foolish. But why do that?

Another time, a dear friend and I were planning to visit an acquaintance who had recently come out of the hospital from a surgical procedure. The convalescing friend was unable to answer the door and had instructed us to come through the front door of her home without knocking. She described her house in detail including the color, house number, and driveway and how the front door would be unlocked. We followed the GPS to her house with a carload of Mylar balloons and a large gift bag filled with goodies we hoped would brighten her day.

We pulled into the curved driveway in front of the two-story grey house and got out of our vehicle, my friend with the bouquet of balloons and me with the gift bag in hand. We let ourselves in through the unlocked front door. The house was quiet and in some bit of a disarray. We called out our friend's name, but no answer followed. Suddenly, a scruffy little dog came out of a side room barking at us in a loud shrilling yelp.

I turned to my friend. "I did not know she had a dog, I thought she had a cat?" I said in a nervous voice.

We continued through the kitchen and into the living room, but still did not find our friend. We looked at each other puzzled and turned to enter a den where we spied an elderly woman, sleeping on a day bed.

She awoke and smiled. "I awake to balloons and two beautiful young women standing in my room. How lucky am I?"

My friend and I stood, mouths open, both in shock! We both asked at the same time if our friend lived there.

The old woman replied, sounding confused, "No, I live here alone."

Confused ourselves, we apologized and hurried back out to the car. We quickly shoved our balloons and gifts into the vehicle and double-checked the GPS. It was then that we discovered that the town we were visiting had several streets with similar names. We found our friends house not too far from the mistaken address and swore a pact to never tell anyone about our mistaken entrance into the house of a stranger. Although my friend and I were horrified about the adventure, we can now laugh openly about our balloon-laden escapade.

One of my finest humorous moments came when I was rushing to do my banking during my lunch half hour. Each Friday, I would hurry to my local bank to make my deposit with hopes of being able to eat my lunch in the car and complete the transaction within the 30 minutes allowed. This particular Friday, I was held up in traffic and flew into the bank parking lot. I jumped out of my car and headed for the door like a woman on a mission and almost cut off a very nice young man who held the door for me to enter. I hurried to the black granite counter to complete my deposit slip and got into line. My transaction complete, I exited the bank and fumbled to get my key fob out of my purse as I approached my car.

As I lifted the handle, the door remained locked. I hit the keyless entry button on my door handle and nothing happened. I then pressed the unlock on my fob several more times to no avail! The keyless entry clearly was not working, and I immediately became agitated and more than a few expletives slipped from my lips. It was then that I noticed the man who had held the door for me, standing behind me with a smile on his face. I figured he wanted to get in his car, so I stepped aside, leaving him enough room to get into the car beside me. He didn't move and I stood there for a brief moment trying to rationalize what he was doing and that's when I noticed it.

I peered through the driver's side window and saw a half-empty water bottle in the console cup holder. I stopped, almost confused. Whose water was that and what had happened to my Diet Coke? I bent closer, cupping my hand over my eyebrows to shield the glare, and noticed a small bag of opened potato chips on the passenger seat.

"Wait a minute," I uttered out loud. "I don't eat potato chips!"

The man chuckled under his breath.

"This is your car, isn't it?" I asked, sheepishly.

He nodded.

I stared down at my feet and then stepped aside as if to usher him to his car.

"I am so sorry. We have the same car, I thought this one was mine."

He graciously accepted my apology. "No harm done, I figured it was something like that."

I quickly hustled over to my car. It immediately opened with the touch of my hand on the keyless entry and I sat inside for a moment and watched the gentleman drive away. I placed my hands on the leather steering wheel and pressed my automatic starter. I felt the smoothness of my leather and inhaled the scent of "sun and sand" from my Yankee Candle Car Jar. Yes, this was my vehicle. The engine hummed and I looked at myself in the rearview mirror. It was then I burst into a loud laugh and kept shaking my head. All the rushing I had done to get back in time for work and I tried to get into another person's car. Needless to say, I was a little late coming back from lunch that day.

When you envision your tapestry from afar, you may, at times, realize that the happiest and brightest times of your picture are surrounded by the days where you let humor into your life. Laughing is always good for the mind, body, and soul. When you visualize what laughter looks like within the perimeter of your masterpiece you will inevitably notice vibrant colors and lively pictures.

They are infectious threads that multiply at a rapid rate. They can touch an infinite number of people in a single instant. When you experience the comedy in a situation, it is your inner light that glows and touches upon the many tapestries around you.

Humor is a gift that should be enjoyed daily. It is okay to laugh at oneself for doing a funny thing. It is not okay, however, to be a joke at everyone's expense. This thread is the piece of our souls that keep us sane and youthful. It is a gift to the past, present, and future of our tapestries. Without this thread, the weaves would become knotted and tight and the colors of our lives are not allowed to dance freely within its body and seams.

Try to love the life you are given while incorporating humor. The threads of humor are simple and free to sew within our images. To embrace them and incorporate them into our daily lives makes even the darkest of times seem lighter and full of hope.

Encourage the humor threads within your tapestry and allow them to weave their magic. Your final picture will bring you joy forever.

THE FINAL GIFT OF THREADS

"We don't accomplish anything in this world alone...and whatever happens is the result of the whole tapestry of one's life and all the weavings of individual threads form one to another that creates something."

~ *Sandra Day O'Connor*

Threads weave their way into our lives for so many reasons. They create many facets of our essence and they develop a bond that depicts a moment or an encounter that is forever sewn into our fabric. We need to be aware of the intensity of their composite. Within each stitch, we contain the ability to help them expand and the capacity to cut them. Events in our lives that occur and can never be changed are forever sewn into our grand picture.

Keep your threads strong, resilient, colorful, and forever expanding. They are a gift to you and to all those you touch. Visualize daily how you want them to develop and make each moment count. Do not waste them on negativity, hatred, jealousy, or envy. They will only wither and decay. Using your threads for positive enlightenment is what will enhance and enrich your tapestry's masterpiece.

May the beauty of your tapestry be as rich as the colors that define it and as deep and strong as the THREADS that bind it.

GLOSSARY

THE THREADS THAT BIND

The composition of the thread is unique to each situation. As in any creation, the materials that are chosen are very significant to the event itself. When picturing your threads remember that they can be as delicate as the strand of a spider's web or as knotted and coarse as twine. Each thread chosen represents the image of the event.

The silken thread is one that is delicate and soft. It is used in times of introspection, the newness of life, or of moments that reflect a delicate interchange between souls. This thread should not be underestimated by its fragile makeup. Some of the simplest of moments are the most binding of ties.

The wispy thread is the thread that represents the ethereal weave. It is of another world composition. It does not usually have its own color or light but reflects the images around it. It is the thread that flows freely and lightly, touching upon the tapestry at key moments.

The base thread is a thread that is strong and resilient. It has a matte sheen and can be seen many times throughout the tapestry. It is resilient and strong and intertwines with other threads to give a solid base to the tapestry.

The knotted thread is coarse and twine-like in texture and feel. It is reflective of moments of great pain, sadness, and emotional discord. It is not a solid colored thread but knotted with other colors to reflect the moment. Although it is the thickest of the threads, it signifies negative moments and does not comprise the strength of the tapestry.

The line thread has a composition likened to fishing line. It is the rarest of threads because of its makeup for strength and absorbing and reflecting light. To catch a glimpse of this thread is magical and the composition in the tapestry requires unique situations. It is easily broken but its effect throughout the tapestry resounds with a vibrancy, all its own.

IN LIVING COLORS

"Colors, like features, follow the changes of the emotions."

~ Pablo Picasso

Colors of the tapestry are unique and personal to each individual. As with the entire concept of threads, there is uniformity to the weave and coloration, but each depiction and image is one of a kind. The colors are defined so that it is easier to visualize the composite of the tapestry being woven and why the colors are so important to the makeup of our final masterpiece.

THE COLOR EVERGREEN

"I am evergreen, and with every passing day, I am becoming younger."

~ Mithun Chakraborty

The color evergreen is the basis of the tapestry. It is the color of life and it is the color of the soul. Evergreen adds a level of vibrancy to our experiences in the creation. It is ever-present in the weave and will be a constant influence in the grand masterpiece even after the soul has crossed through the veil and continues its journey in the life beyond.

Whether a life has been given the gift of longevity or only a brief span on earth, the quantitative and qualitative measure of its beauty is unaffected. Each life produces vibrant colors. Evergreen is most present because it represents the soul itself, which is innately a beacon of strength, hope, courage, and love.

THE COLOR RED

Red is the first color of spring. It's the real color of rebirth. Of Beginning"

~Andie Condie

In times of deep love, intense anger, or passion, the color red weaves its way into the fabric of the tapestry. Red can represent a spiritual nature such as the red of the cardinal, which for many, is seen as a harbinger of messages and signs from heaven. But it can also be seen as anger and be associated with passion and fear. It can represent a burning desire to be a part of something. Whites and blues change their forms when mingled with the intensity of red. When imagining the intensity of the color within our own picture we can almost see red because of its ability to pulse with a mystic flow. Consider the red threads in your own tapestry representing the heartbeat of your life, weaving and flowing within your picture and giving it life and emotion.

THE COLOR YELLOW

"There is a sun, a light that for want of a better word I can only call yellow, pale sulphur yellow, pale golden citron. How lovely yellow is!

~ *Vincent Van Gogh*

The color yellow is the merriest of the tapestry. The one that brightens the darks and brings forth the warmth of our lives. It is the color that can turn a garden green, a special moment warm, or a mood change light and joyful. It is the most appreciative of the color in our tapestries. Yellows have the ability to soften with its tenderness and cheer with brightness.

The yellow lemon ball of the sunrises and sunsets represents the opening of our day and all of its potential and the closing of each day with all of its accomplishments. It is that thread color that enhances our tapestries with the endearment and spiritual openness to greet each day with unmasked potential and embracing all that is bestowed upon us.

THE COLOR BLUE

"If the sight of the blue skies fills you with joy, if a blade of grass springing up in the fields has power to move you, if the simple things of nature have a message that you understand, rejoice, for your soul is alive."

~ *Eleonora Duse*

Blues have a calming hue about them. They cool or temper us throughout our life. Think of the moment when you notice the sky, blue and endless. The thread commences light, wispy and delicate. The depth of the blue in the sky gives feelings of serenity and peace. As you peer deeper into the depth you feel enlightened and your strand becomes stronger. At that moment you realize it is not yours alone, that you are at one with the universe and sharing it with the multitudes.

THE COLOR BROWN

"I cannot pretend to feel impartial about the colors. I rejoice with the brilliant ones and am genuinely sorry for the poor browns."

~ *Sir Winston Churchill*

The color brown is not to be defined by its simple hue. It is the color that signifies stability and forms the foundation of the tapestry. When we imagine the browns of our lives, we perceive times of quiet. Through this color, the weaves of stability to our home life and family are enhanced. It is the wood in our fireplace that allows the yellow to warm our home as we are comforted by its glow. It is the earth that allows our grass to grow green, our flowers to bloom or house to stand. So many times, brown is overlooked because of its muddy reflection in the tapestry. But it is that very brown that sustains us and our picture and allows our foundation to grow. The most unnoticed color of our tapestries because of its lack of brilliance, brown remains an important part of our foundation through strength and fortitude and keeping our path steady and firm.

THE COLOR PURPLE

"Soon it got dusk, a grapy dusk, a purple dusk over tangerine groves and long melon fields; the sun the color of pressed grapes, slashed with burgundy red, the fields the color of love and Spanish mysteries."

~ *Jack Kerouac*

Purple bathes our world in a majestic color. Its appearance in our tapestry is viewed with a richness that enhances the depth of whatever it touches. The vastness of the night sky or the awestruck beauty of a mountain top, purple enriches our picture with regal splendor and gives character to our tapestry.

THE COLOR GREY

"Grey has no agenda....Grey has the ability that no other colour has, to make the invisible visible."

~ *Roma Tearne*

The color grey casts calm and reflective hues into its vastness, and yet often relates more in terms of dreary moments or sad feelings. Shades of grey contain beauty as well. It is the color of the ocean as it reflects the darkness of the sky, moving and flowing with a somber motion. It is the chromaticity of the clouds before the raindrops fall, providing us with precipitation and shade. Grey completes our tapestries. It is the color that can cast shadows on our lives in the form of storms and dissipate so gently so that we may usher in the more vibrant hues like those of the rainbow.

THE RAINBOW

"Let me, O let me bathe my soul in colours; let me swallow the sunset and drink the rainbow."

~ *Kahlil Gibran*

The colors of the rainbow represent an array of feelings and textures that blend together in one grand picture. There is a uniqueness that can be derived from the colors of the rainbow as the colors create a whole new spectrum of hues. For most of its colors represent something spiritual and happy. The rainbow has been seen to represent a promise from God, a feeling of hope and an avenue for finding the mystical pot of gold. The colors individually represent specific feelings or experiences, but when melded together have an inspirational connotation.

THE COLOR PINK

"Sunrise paints the sky with pinks and the sunset with peaches. Cool to warm. So is the progression from childhood to old age."

~ *Vera Nazarian*

The color pink in your tapestry is the mixture of emotions and senses. It is a blend that magically connects our tapestries to so many moments in time through softness, comfort, love, and feminine strength and beauty. It is the ever-present color of love and warmth born out of the mixture of the fiery passion of red and the purity of the color white. Light pink represents the color of newness, as in a newborn baby girl. The deeper hues reflect a maturity as it ages through the continuity of time. It can also have a delicate nature to it such as the petals on a carnation or rose. When looking at a beautiful summer sky, or late winter sky, the hues of pinks can be the most spiritual of all.

THE COLOR SILVER

"I don't want a rainbow... Rainbows have too many colors and none of them receive the appreciation they deserve... I'd prefer a fading red or a striking golden, a shimmering silver or a sober blue... Ruling the sunset sky alone!"

~ *Debalina Haldar*

The color silver in the tapestry of life is a color that represents wisdom and strength. Silver is a precious metal and is used in rare moments in our picture when the value of its worth can be applied. The silver can be the hue in the color grey, reflecting the age and maturing of our lives and those around us. It can also be that glimmering sheen that flits across our tapestries indicating rare and valuable moments. It represents enlightenment in our lives and grows thicker and stronger as the years go on. It is precious to behold and requires respect and admiration to use it. Silver has the capacity to color our tapestries with majestic quality, internal reflection, and the sagacity that comes within our elder years.

THE COLOR GOLD

"I wear myself out and struggle with the sun. And what a sun here! It would be necessary to paint here with gold and gemstones. It is wonderful."

~ *Claude Monet*

Gold is the color that brightens our tapestries the most. It enriches our moments, enlivens our souls, and gives the tapestry the embodiment of worth. It is a rare color in our creation. Gold allows us to experience pure moments of greatness, happiness, pleasure, and deep awakening. The threads are woven in and out of the other colors to give a sheen of magical occurrences in our lives. Gold is invaluable to have because of its uniqueness to the grand picture. It is fleeting and profound all at once and when reviewing the threads throughout our tapestries we see how treasured those gold moments were. They bring life to our ever-expanding tapestries and showcase our most poignant and dear happenings in the glitter of gold thread. Golden moments are those moments of great treasure, especially when realizing that the treasure isn't just in jewels or money, but in the deep love and respect of the ones that meant the most to us.

THE COLOR BLACK

"When you photograph people in color, you photograph their clothes. But when you photograph people in black and white, you photograph their souls!"

~ *Ted Grant*

Significant moments of black and white are interwoven in the beauty of our lives' pictures. Although black signifies death or unhappy moments, it is the color or basis for producing the strength and depth of life. It can be intertwined with the other colors and may often be the color within a knotted thread. Black inevitability finds its way into every tapestry.

If you were to envision a forest fire that has decimated the woodlands and all its exterior foliage, it is within the rubble, ash, and soot that a person would recognize the simple little green branch or leaf growing out of its destruction. That is what our tapestries capture, the strength to sustain our bodies, minds, and souls. It allows us to see through the darkness that can engulf us and allow the glint of light or bloom of life to stand out among it.

THE COLOR WHITE

"White is not a mere absence of color; it is a shining and affirmative thing, as fierce as red, as definite as black. God paints in many colors; but He never paints so gorgeously, I had almost said so gaudily, as when He paints in white."

~ *G.K. Chesterton*

The white of our tapestries is also predominant within its landscape. White is often viewed as a pure, untouched color that reflects our newness and spiritual awakening. It can enrich the other colors with its purity, making their hues softer. White is our blank page, our openness to what is to be, and reflects the light of our transition into the next world, heaven.

The Threads of Sunrises and Sunsets

When was the last time you saw a sunrise or a sunset? Did you take the time to watch it? What does it make you think of or feel?

The Threads of Moments in Time

Have you ever had a moment when the delicacy and brevity of life have really hit you?

The Threads Cast

Can you think of a time when you've reached out to someone about something via social media or email and it formed an impactful connection?

The Threads of Living with Regret

We all have threads of regret. How often do they make an appearance in your life?

The Threads of Commitment

Have there been any tasks or commitments you've agreed to take on that were incredibly difficult? Were you able to complete those tasks? If not, what stood in your way?

The Thread of Divine Intervention

Do you believe that sometimes we meet people or have spiritual experiences because we were meant to?

The Threads of Dreams

Have you ever had a dream that you felt was trying to tell or show you something?

The Threads of Clarity

Have you ever had a moment of profound clarity? Maybe the answer to a question finally arrived in your mind. Or maybe you were able to make a big decision with ease? How did it feel to have that clarity?

The Threads of Nature

Have you ever witnessed a movement or example in nature that took your breath away? How did you feel in that moment? How do you feel now when you recall that moment?

The Threads of New Experiences

Have you ever taken up a new endeavor or hobby and found it brought you great joy? Or maybe it didn't work out the way you thought? Would you consider it a learning experience either way?

The Threads of the Woven Words

Do you find that you often think about what you are saying before you voice the words?

The Threads of Acceptance

Have you ever just had to accept something about yourself or your life and then used it as a way to grow and become stronger in other ways?

The Threads of Loving What You Have

What do you have in your life that makes you truly happy? Do you take time to really appreciate the good stuff in your life?

The Threads of Pain

When you think about the pain you have experienced in your life, do you ever see a silver lining? Has that pain helped you to grow or understand yourself or another better?

The Threads of Good Intentions

Have you ever taken the time to do something nice for someone else just because you knew it would make them feel better? Have you ever had someone do something nice out of the blue for you?

The Threads of Time

In your day-to-day existence, do you take time to just breath and feel rooted in your place and space in time? Do you feel like you are constantly hurrying from one place and one task to the next?

The Threads of Adventure

Have you ever done anything that people insisted you were out of your mind to try? Did you do it anyway? How did it work out?

The Threads of Being Good to Yourself

Do you take the time to do nice things for yourself? If so, what's your favorite "I love me time!" thing to do?

The Thread of New Souls

Have you ever given something you really love to someone else because you knew they needed it? If so, how did that make you feel?

The Threads of Beauty of The Beholder

When it comes to beauty, how do you define it? What makes someone beautiful?

The Threads of Love

What does the thread of love look like to you? When it appears in your tapestry, how does it make you feel?

The Threads of Times Past

Have you ever owned or discovered an antique or artifact that you felt connected to?

The Threads of the Child Within You

Do you think that there is always a child-like part of us that never grows up? Do you allow that part of you to emerge or do you tend to contain your inner child?

The Threads of Reminders

Do you have a gratitude jar? Do you make a point to give thanks for the people, things, and events in your life?

The Threads of Friendships

Think about one of your friends. How did you meet? Were you instant friends? What helped connect you to this person?

The Threads of Connections

Have you ever had a psychic reading? Or maybe just had someone say something or do something that you felt was a message or a sign?

The Threads of Kindred Spirits

Do you have a kindred or one of a kind connection with a special person? If so, how would you describe that connection?

The Threads of Saying Goodbye

Have you ever had to say goodbye to a family pet? Or someone else that you care about? Do you ever feel like they are still around you?

The Threads of Disappointment

Have you ever been disappointed about something only to later realize it was the best thing that could have happened?

The Threads of Following Your Own Heart

If you could follow your heart right now, what would you do?

The Threads of Being Open

Has there been an occasion when you followed a calling to do something and you later realized that it was exactly what you were supposed to do?

The Thread of Our Gifts

What gifts do you have? Do you wish you could use them more?

The Threads of Despair

Do you think that these moments make you feel more connected or less connected to others?

The Threads of Emotional Growth

Have you ever met someone or seen something that completely snapped you out of your routine or changed your entire perspective about something?

The Threads of Overcoming

Do you know someone who has struggle with addiction? Are they seeking help? How has it impacted you and those around you?

The Threads of Origin

What does the thread of your origin look like?

The Threads of Goodness

Who in your life embodies the thread of goodness?

The Threads of Mindfulness

Take a look around you. What do you see that grounds you? What do you see that you are thankful for?

The Threads of Revisiting Pain

Have you ever drawn on your own painful experiences to help others?

The Threads of Our Own Paths

Is there someone in your life that you traveled life's path with for a time and then separated

The Threads of Intense Emotion

Do you think intense emotions impact our ability to learn? To understand others?

The Threads of Lasting Importance

Is there a time when you saw something one way and someone else thought of it in a completely different light?

The Threads of Humor

Do you think you have the ability to laugh at yourself?

The Final Gift of Threads

What thread has resonated with you the most? What colors do you see in your tapestry?

A Note From the Author

Thank you for reading Threads. If you enjoyed this book, would you please consider rating and reviewing it at **www.amazon.com**?

For more information please visit me at the following:

https://www.judithcosby.com

https://www.facebook.com/JudithAnnCosby

https://www.linkedin.com/in/judith-cosby-799079124

CPSIA information can be obtained
at www.ICGtesting.com
Printed in the USA
BVHW031713020719
552502BV00001B/53/P